your

From Area codes 01923 or 020:
Renewals: 01923 471373
Textphone: 01923 471599
From the rest of Herts:
Renewals: 01438 737373
Textphone: 01438 737599
www.hertsdirect.org/libraries

Hertfordshire

hamlyn

your child's dog

Andrea McHugh

How to help
your kids care
for their pets

An Hachette Livre UK Company

First published in Great Britain in 2007 by Hamlyn,
a division of Octopus Publishing Group Ltd,
2–4 Heron Quays, London E14 4JP

ISBN-13: 978-0-600-61594-1
ISBN-10: 0-600-61594-4

A CIP catalogue record for this book is available from the
British Library.

Printed and bound in China

10 9 8 7 6 5 4 3 2 1

Notes

The advice given here should not be used as a substitute for that of a
veterinary surgeon. No dogs or puppies were harmed in the making
of this book.

Unless the information given in this book is specifically for female dogs,
dogs are referred to throughout as 'he'. Unless otherwise specified, the
information is applicable equally to male and female dogs.

Contents

Introduction 6

1 Can we get a dog? 8

2 Preparing for the puppy 18

3 The first few days 32

4 Routine matters 46

5 Growing pains 62

6 Training for kids 72

7 Health and safety 98

8 What if? 110

Index 124

Acknowledgements 128

Introduction

There is no doubt that a dog can bring a huge amount of pleasure and fun to the whole family. Having a pet like a dog will also help your child learn important lessons about being responsible for the health and wellbeing of another living creature. However, looking after a dog properly requires time, commitment and effort, and it will change the way your family lives. This is something that is not always easy to convey to children. If you are a parent or guardian and you find yourself being put under pressure to buy a dog, then this is the book for you.

This book has been written to give you, the responsible adult, an understanding of exactly what is involved in caring for a dog, and the words to explain things in ways that children will understand. Simply telling a child not to carry a puppy everywhere like a toy will probably go in one ear and out the other. After all, a cute puppy looks just like a toy, and a determined child will just find his wriggling endearing. However, if you can explain the reasons why a dog doesn't like to be carried (because he feels insecure and vulnerable without the use of his legs to run away from danger), you will help even a young child to imagine how the puppy is feeling.

Using simple step-by-step instructions, this book also shows how children can be involved in every aspect of looking after their pet, so that you don't need to worry that you will be left with all the chores as soon as the novelty wears off. As well as demonstrating how to get your child stuck into the routine care, such as feeding, exercising and grooming, there's also lots of information about teaching children to train a puppy from scratch. Helping your child train a dog to sit, walk on a lead and roll over will strengthen the bond between child and puppy – and also take much of the responsibility for training out of your hands.

You'll also discover how to involve your child in the less exciting aspects of dog ownership, such as checking for fleas, bathing and visiting the vet. Each stage of a dog's life has its own challenges, and your child will need help to learn how to deal with these and to behave in a way that will ensure that the puppy remains happy and well as he becomes an adult.

As a first step, you need to decide as a family whether you are able to offer a home to a dog or whether it would be better to defer the decision for a while. When you are certain that you are ready and able to become a dog-owning family, the next stage is to do your research and decide on the best type of dog for you. And once you've chosen your puppy, you need to prepare your home and your children for the new arrival. This includes discussing how responsibility will be allocated among different members of the family and making sure the house and garden are a puppy-friendly zone.

Once you have brought the dog home, you are faced with a whole new set of questions and potential problems. How can your child and dog play safely together? How do you deal with bad behaviour from puppy or child? And how do you answer all those awkward or embarrassing questions? Look out for the 'Question time' boxes, which pose all the questions that children commonly ask. In each case, you'll find an explanation of the underlying issues as well as a sample answer couched in terms that your child should find easy to understand.

Learning as much as possible about canine behaviour, and about the way that dogs communicate with each other and with their owners, means that you and your family will get maximum enjoyment from your dog. And, after all, having fun together is what owning a dog is all about.

chapter 1

Can we get a dog?

This chapter is all about deciding whether you are ready and able to welcome a puppy into your family. 'Please can I have a dog?' is probably a request that you've heard quite often. Most children would love to own a puppy, dreaming of cuddling him every night and having fun together. Unfortunately, they don't usually think much beyond that, and their knowledge tends to be gleaned from fictional characters, like Scooby Doo and Snoopy. These cartoon dogs are heroic, talking animals, who are more than capable of looking after themselves and their owners. The reality, of course, is that a dog needs a lot of care and attention.

Under pressure

Children decide that they want a dog for all sorts of reasons, which range from peer pressure to a new film or book that's just come out featuring a doggy hero. They can exert significant pressure on their parents, and busy working people often give in through guilt or the desire for a quiet life. Unfortunately, dogs who are acquired in these circumstances often have to be re-homed when the novelty wears off and the children's initial enthusiasm fades.

It's no use telling your children, 'You'll have to walk the dog every day and feed it and groom it.' A desperate child will automatically say, 'I will! I promise! Please, please! I'll look after it for the rest of my life and love you for ever.' Does this sound familiar? There are wonderful advantages for the whole family in owning a dog, and some of these are described later in the book (see pages 12–13, for example), but it's still important to do your homework thoroughly before you buy one. When you know exactly what is involved, you can decide as a family whether you are in a position to bring a dog into your lives and provide him with a good home.

Fast forward

Before you agree that your child can have a puppy and start to bask in the glow of gratitude and their assurances that you are the best parent in the world, take a few moments to think about the time when that appealing puppy is a large, boisterous hound. Imagine a wet, dark, wintry morning. Your child has some homework to finish, and, in any case, you are not keen that she should be outdoors in the dark, even with a dog. So, it's down to you to put on your coat and venture outdoors. The problem is that nobody has trained the dog, who won't come back when he's called. You miss breakfast and are late for work. As if that's not bad enough, when you get home you find that the dog has destroyed your favourite cushion and chewed the leg of a chair. You stare open-mouthed – Scooby Doo and Snoopy never behaved like that.

Thankfully, careful planning and the commitment of the whole family will enable you to avoid days like that. Learning to share with your child the care of your dog and responsibility for it will allow you all to enjoy the loving companionship of a loyal and well-behaved family friend.

What a dog owner
provides

Considering what a dog requires to be happy and healthy is the first step to deciding whether you can provide a good home for one. You should also think about your own lifestyle and how it might be affected by having a dog. Like a new baby, a puppy turns family life upside down, and your responsibility for the animal will continue for many years after he has been trained.

Your circumstances

As an initial step, think about where you live, how many children you have (or are planning to have), your child's personality and the time you all will have available to spend with the dog. Remember to factor in any time spent on other activities, such as football, ballet lessons or music practice, which may have to be forfeited. You should also calculate how much of the household budget you can comfortably afford for a dog's care, including regular visits to the vet.

When your child first asks if he can have a puppy, it is worth sitting down together and making a checklist of a dog's basic requirements. It is important to explain to your child that a dog needs to be given everything on this list if he is to be happy and healthy – and not just the fun-sounding aspects like play and cuddles. Most children will find that words like 'training' and 'socialization' sound exceptionally dull, but do point out to them that these aspects of a dog's care can actually turn out to be the most fun and most rewarding.

Can you supply these?

- [ ] Fresh water
- [ ] Good-quality dog food
- [ ] Shelter from the elements
- [ ] Exercise and play
- [ ] Grooming
- [ ] Freedom from pain
- [ ] Routine veterinary care
- [ ] Socialization (getting your dog used to strange noises and people)
- [ ] Training
- [ ] Mental stimulation
- [ ] Affection and companionship

How much time?

The main thing a dog needs from you and your child is time. Puppies vary enormously in how long it takes them to become house-trained and settled into a new home, but this is a stage that you must all be prepared to work on. Training basic obedience and, most importantly, teaching your child how to handle and work with the dog will also take time and patience, and you also need to think about the time you will spend on general care, including walking, playing, feeding and grooming.

Spontaneous sleepovers at friends' houses will become a thing of the past, because you will always have to consider the dog and make arrangements for his care. This can be a shock to a family that has never owned a pet before, and it is important to consider whether everyone is willing to accept these constraints.

How much money?

Dogs can be expensive, particularly if they become sick and need veterinary treatment, and budgeting for an annual or monthly pet insurance policy is important. If you are planning to buy a pedigree, expect to pay much more than you would for a crossbreed or mongrel.

Other costs

* Boarding fees if you go away on holiday
* Dog food
* Essential items, such as a bed, collar, lead and identity tag and food and water bowls
* Microchipping
* A pet passport if you intend to travel with your dog
* Dog training classes

How long?

Barring illness and accidents, large and giant breeds, such as Great Danes and German Shepherd Dogs, live for eight to ten years, while smaller breeds, such as Jack Russell Terriers and Yorkshire Terriers, can live into their late teens. Your child may well be leaving home to go to college when the dog is still in its prime and you could become the sole carer at a time when you may well be looking forward to freedom from responsibilities. On the positive side, having a dog can help to fill the gap when a child leaves the nest, and the routine of caring for him can relieve stress and provide companionship.

ABOVE LEFT: Regular grooming is essential to keep your dog's coat clean and tangle-free.

ABOVE RIGHT: Border Collies were originally bred to herd sheep and need lots of exercise and stimulation.

OPPOSITE: Leading the puppy outside to toilet after feeding is one easy way in which your child can take responsibility for his care.

Tip to parents

To help you prepare a budget, visit your vet and find out how much his annual vaccinations, flea treatments and check-ups are likely to cost, then allow extra for emergencies.

Right reasons
for getting a puppy

Parents should never feel obliged to get a dog to salve a guilty conscience because they are too busy to spend time with their children. Ultimately, they won't have time for the dog, either. Similarly, buying a dog to cheer up a child after the parents separate or divorce will help only if the parent with whom the child lives has sufficient time and money for the extra commitment.

Benefits

As well as providing an immense amount of fun, owning a dog and taking responsibility for it offers a child valuable life lessons, including developing empathy and concern for the welfare of others, and dealing with loss. Research has shown that there are also many other benefits from owning a pet. For example, studies have found that:

- Children with pets tend to be fitter and more sociable than those without.
- Autistic children with pets show more pro-social behaviours and less autistic behaviours than those without pets.
- Teenage pet owners living in deprived areas are more content and have better relationships with adults than their peers without pets.
- Children exposed to pets during the first year of life have a lower frequency of allergic rhinitis and asthma.

Disadvantages

When you are considering getting a dog, remember that there are several disadvantages, the most serious of which is probably lack of freedom. You must always arrange for the dog's care when you go away or are likely to be delayed, and, if you already lead a very busy life,

LEFT: Choose a quiet time of year to bring your puppy home (avoid Christmas or birthdays), so that he can settle in with minimum fuss.

OPPOSITE ABOVE: If you have a baby, it may be a good idea to choose a gentle, small breed. Dogs should never be left unsupervised with small children.

with lots of other commitments, it might be better to defer getting a dog until the whole family has more time.

Don't forget that a dog will add to the family budget. Vet's bills, food, insurance and boarding fees when you are away on holiday can be significant items, so think carefully before taking on the extra burden.

Some people are phobic or allergic to animals. Think about how you would cope with this if you introduced a dog into your home. Also, if you are very house-proud you should think about how you would deal with the inevitable mess that having a dog will bring.

Baby love

Some children are born into households where there is already a family pet, and, if steps are taken to make sure that the dog doesn't become jealous or isolated, there is no reason why significant problems should arise. However, buying a puppy when you have a new baby is probably not a good idea, even if you think it would be 'nice for them grow up together'. Juggling the very demanding care of a new puppy and a baby may well mean that someone will miss out.

If you would like to have a dog but are uncertain whether your children have reached an appropriate age, consider how much responsibility you expect them to assume for the dog's wellbeing (see pages 14–15).

Question time

Q *Can I have a puppy for my birthday?*
Much as this may be your child's dream present, it is better to wait until after the actual day. Explain this to your child, but give a gift-wrapped dog collar, lead or bowl as reassurance that the dream will come true.

A The puppy won't be very happy to arrive on your birthday. There would be too much going on and he would be scared. All the visitors, loud noises and party games would mean he wouldn't get enough rest. Let's make a list of things we need for the puppy and ask people to get those for your birthday. We can get the dog later.

Q *When can I have a dog then?*
Patience is not usually a strong point with children. The beginning of the autumn term will give the dog time to settle in while the children are at school.

A The best time is probably after the summer holidays, because we'll all have lots of time for him then. You can enjoy playing with the dog before and after school, and he can rest while you are in classes.

Who will care for the puppy?

Before you commit to getting a dog, decide who is going to be responsible for the different aspects of his care. Your discussion should cover responsibilities such as feeding, exercising and grooming, as well as cleaning up after the puppy. Encourage the children to draw up a rota themselves, so that everyone knows exactly who would do what job and when.

ABOVE LEFT: Even very small children can take responsibility for keeping the puppy's water bowl topped up.

ABOVE RIGHT: Giving the puppy lots of affection is one duty that your children won't want to shirk!

OPPOSITE: Older children will enjoy feeding the dog, under adult supervision.

Sharing the load

There will be plenty of volunteers for the fun stuff, like playing with the puppy, but children may not be so keen to help when it comes to tidying up or doing the 'dirty' jobs, like grooming. Allocating particular tasks to everyone in the family provides an opportunity for them to bond with the dog and will help the puppy become a real member of the family.

Take into account your children's ages and their physical and mental abilities and always supervise them. Even toddlers can be allocated simple tasks, such as fetching the dog's food from the cupboard when it is time to feed him, and putting it away again afterwards. Older children can accompany an adult on walks, participate in training, go to puppy classes, learn how to groom the dog and help with many other tasks.

Inevitably there will be some mess involved in keeping a dog. You can expect muddy paws on the kitchen floor and hairs on the carpet, so decide who will help clean up. If it is always the same person who does this, it may cause resentment. Agreeing to take responsibility in turns, perhaps on a daily or weekly basis, will help to avoid turning cleaning into an issue.

Question time

Q *If I've got homework and football practice, will I still have to walk the dog?*
Encouraging children to help care for their dog every day, no matter what the weather or other activities, helps them to develop a sense of responsibility. If necessary, visit your veterinary surgery and ask a member of staff to explain the importance of a specific task, such as grooming, and how failure to do this properly will affect the dog's wellbeing.

A The dog will still need walking but perhaps we could do two jobs at once, such as walking to football practice and taking the dog with us or walking him to school and back each day. If you don't want to be involved in caring for the dog maybe we should get one later, when you are less busy.

There are lots of ways in which children can be involved in looking after the dog:

- Getting dog food out at meal times and putting it away again; older children can feed the dog under supervision before and after school.
- Washing, drying and putting away the dog's food and water dishes.
- Checking and refilling the water bowls.
- Fetching the dog's grooming kit and putting it away; older children can learn how to groom the dog.
- Hanging up his collar and lead tidily.
- Helping to do a weekly health check of paws, teeth, eyes and fur.
- Keeping the dog's toy box tidy and clearing away their own toys so that the dog doesn't think they are his.
- Spending some time playing with the dog each day.
- Helping to walk the dog and washing and drying muddy paws afterwards.
- Learning how to mop a muddy floor and vacuum up dog hair from the carpets and the furniture.

Doing your
puppy
research

There is a lot you can do as a family to prepare for owning a dog. Start by doing as much research as possible into the different dog breeds, in order to find out which would be the best type for your family. Take into account where you live, how much space you have and how much free time everyone will have to spend on the dog.

Sources of information

The internet is a great resource, with numerous pedigree breed sites available that allow you to see what the dogs will look like as puppies and adults and find out whether they are low or high maintenance. Your library will also stock a range of books on different breeds.

Make a note of the breeds that interest you and visit some dog shows to see them in action. Most people are only too happy to talk about their dogs, and as long as they are not waiting to go into a competition or are busy getting their dogs ready to show, you should be able to find out useful information, such as how good they are as family pets, how easy they are to look after and whether they require lots of exercise.

Helping hands

If your neighbour has a dog, ask if your children can help walk him occasionally. This is a good way of finding out if they will be as committed to walking a dog on a cold, wet morning as they are on a sunny afternoon. Ask your neighbour to explain what is involved and make sure that all the negative aspects are discussed, as well as the positive ones.

Many canine rescue centres and shelters rely on volunteers to help care for their dogs. Your family may enjoy becoming involved for a couple

LEFT: If you have access to the internet, you will be able to visit many different websites about dog breeds and dog ownership.

OPPOSITE: Dogs have to be walked in cold, wet weather, too. Ask your neighbours if your child can come along whenever they walk their dogs – whatever the weather.

of hours each weekend, and as a bonus the dogs will benefit from the extra socialization with children, making it easier for staff to re-home them. Being involved with rescue dogs can help your family decide what kind of dog they like best as well as getting first-hand experience of the work involved. Statistics show that more dogs are re-homed during the first year of ownership than at any other time, simply because the families concerned didn't realize what having a dog really involved.

Saving plan

You can help your children develop a sense of commitment by encouraging them to do extra jobs around the home and save their pocket money to buy something for the dog, such as a collar, or to add to a dog-buying fund.

Question time

Q *Why do I have to learn so much about dogs before we get a puppy?*
The more children know, the more interested they should become. If their enthusiasm wanes at this stage, you can assume that the desire to have a dog is a passing whim and decide not to pursue dog ownership any further at the moment. Some of the learning activities you could try include: picking up leaflets from your veterinary surgery; joining the junior branch of your national Kennel Club; visiting dog-training classes to see a variety of dog activities, such as flyball, agility and obedience training; talking to as many dog owners as possible, both adult and children; subscribing to a dog-care magazine; and making a list of local dog breeders and arranging visits.

A Learning about dogs is fun, and the more everyone in the family knows, the better we can look after the dog and the happier he will be.

chapter 2

Preparing for the puppy

You've thought hard about how a dog will change family life and you've started your research into the different types and breeds of dog. Now it's time to find the puppy! This chapter explains what to consider when buying your dog and it also explores how to prepare your family for the arrival of a new member. This includes creating a set of rules for both the family and the puppy, and explaining to your child about life from a dog's point-of-view. Even the most good-natured dog has his breaking point and your child will need to respect that.

Which dogs make good family pets?

Some breeds, such as the Border Collie, which was originally bred to herd sheep, require a lot of mental and physical stimulation to keep them occupied. Other breeds, such as the Golden Retriever, which responds well to training, are more placid and have a reputation for being excellent family pets. Toy dogs, such as the Chihuahua, look appealing but can be difficult to house-train and may not enjoy the constant attention of children. Large breeds can be gentle giants, but because of their size may accidentally knock over small children.

While any breed has the potential to be a good family pet, when there are children involved you need to find a puppy who can cope happily with family life and who is safe with children. Consider whether the breed is suitable for your children's age, bearing in mind that a large or strong dog may be difficult for your child to handle. A small but temperamental breed may also not be the best choice for boisterous children. Think about why your child wants a dog – is he looking for companionship or entertainment, for example?

You also need to take your own needs into consideration. Avoid giant breeds if you can't afford the upkeep and do not go for long-haired breeds if hairs on the carpet will drive you

mad. Be honest about the time you will have available to spend with your dog.

If you are buying a pedigree dog (see pages 20–21), you can find out information about the dog's characteristics and behaviour by researching the breed thoroughly and talking to breeders. Consider what the dog was originally bred to do – herding, retrieving, hunting and so on.

Adult or puppy?

Most children would love to have a cute puppy, and one of the benefits of this is that they will be involved in every stage of the dog's development and training. However, puppies are a lot of work for the first few weeks, so you must be prepared to commit extra time and patience.

Sometimes an adult dog becomes available who would make a perfect family pet. Perhaps a family you know are emigrating or their personal circumstances have changed and they are no longer able to care for the dog properly. If this dog ticks all the boxes on your wish list and has already proved to be a good family pet, your children may be thrilled to take him on. A word of caution though: it is stressful for any dog to go to a new home, so be prepared for a period of adjustment.

Where to buy
your new puppy

Once you have decided to get a dog, it can be tempting to buy the first one you see. However, before you make a final choice, there are some other points to consider. Do you want a pedigree or a non-pedigree dog? Both have their advantages and disadvantages. And where will you find your dog? Bear in mind that pet shops and puppy farms are not the best sources.

Pedigree or non-pedigree?

There are advantages to buying a pedigree puppy. You will be able to meet the breeder and the dog's parents, so will be able to predict the dog's appearance as an adult as well as behaviour traits and potential health problems. The dog will be fully vaccinated and socialized. You will also receive pedigree certificates and a family tree, and your dog will be able to compete in pedigree dog shows. There is also a downside, however: pedigree breeds can be expensive, they are not always immediately available and some are susceptible to health problems. Some pedigree breeds may even be targeted by thieves.

The alternative is to buy a crossbreed, for which two different pure-bred parents were mated, or a randomly bred dog, which is usually

ABOVE: A small breed, such as a Dachshund, can be less intimidating for small children than a larger size of dog.

OPPOSITE: Friendly, playful and kind, Golden Retrievers are a popular choice for families.

LEFT: Border Terriers are affectionate, good-tempered and always ready to play.

the result of an accidental mating. These are less expensive and often more hardy than pedigree dogs and less likely to be stolen. Non-pedigree dogs are also easy to obtain and visually unique. However, problems may arise if the dog's family history is unknown. There is no guarantee how it will look as an adult and it may be susceptible to health problems. It may also not be vaccinated.

Questions to ask the breeder

Before you buy a pedigree puppy draw up a list of questions. You will have to answer some questions, too, because reputable breeders are extremely fussy about re-homing their dogs. Questions you should ask include:

- When were the puppies born?
- Where have they been kept? (In the home is preferable to outside in a kennel.)
- Can we see both parents?
- Were any pre-breeding tests done that show the puppies could develop disease?

- What are their temperaments like?
- Are they used to other people and pets?
- Have they been handled much?
- Are they high- or low-maintenance dogs?
- Are they vaccinated and microchipped?
- Are they insured?

Where to buy?

Your children may be drawn to pet shops but these are not the best places to get a puppy, because you cannot be certain about the dog's background. Some puppies are bred in poor conditions on puppy farms and may, as a consequence, suffer health problems later. Buying a dog from a registered, reputable breeder is a much better option. Animal welfare centres are also always full of dogs in need of good homes. Be prepared to undergo a home assessment and answer questions about your lifestyle, to help the charity suggest the dogs that are best suited to your family. Avoid puppy farms and unscrupulous breeders, and never, ever buy on impulse.

A puppy's place
in the family
hierarchy

Before your new puppy comes home it is a good idea to think about where he is going to fit in to the existing family hierarchy. Discuss this with your children and ask them to think about how they should react to the newcomer. It is important that the puppy realizes from the start that he is not, and never will be, the top dog in his pack, which consists of members of your household.

Pampered pooches

Initially, the puppy is bound to be the centre of attention in the household, but if this continues for too long it can become stressful for the animal. Stressed dogs can exhibit behavioural problems, which may manifest in different ways, depending on his personality type. House-training problems, constant barking, chewing or self-harm, such as obsessive over-licking of fur, can all be symptoms of stress. In addition, over-pampered pooches do not make great family pets because they become demanding and disruptive.

Top dogs

The puppy must be taught that the adults in the house are at the top of the family hierarchy, with the children after that, followed by any existing pets and, finally, at the bottom of the pile, him. Dominant behaviour that can be appealing in a little puppy will not be acceptable in a mature dog. If a dog is allowed to assume the role of top

Do!

- Arrange for the puppy to be neutered or spayed as soon as possible
- Feed the puppy after other family members and other pets
- Allocate a sleeping area for the puppy
- Be consistent with rules
- Enrol in a puppy training class

Don't! encourage your child to . . .

- Feed treats indiscriminately
- Play chasing or tug-of-war games

ABOVE: Holding a toy up high can be perceived by the dog as an invitation to jump up and grab it.

RIGHT: If your children say 'no' to the puppy and stop playing with him as soon as he nips or chews, he will soon learn to behave.

OPPOSITE: If you don't want your dog on the sofa, make sure he knows that his place is always on the floor and don't let the children allow him to break the rules.

dog in the house, he will allocate himself the best chair, help himself to anything he wants to eat, including from your children's plates, take ownership of the children's toys, and become quite intimidating as he growls warnings at anyone who walks past him. Many of these dogs are eventually labelled 'bad dogs' and end up in a re-homing centre, where, at best, they undergo a lengthy behaviour therapy programme before being re-homed. At worst, they will be euthanized.

The only way to avoid this difficult situation developing is to create a set of family house rules from day one and adhere to them. It is not necessary to resort to shouting or turn into some kind of autocratic monster. Simply being firm, fair and consistent about when and where the puppy is fed and where he is allowed to sit and sleep, and immediately stopping any games that encourage the dog to think he can be dominant over the children, is sufficient. For example, feed the family before the puppy gets his dinner, don't allow the puppy to walk through doorways in front of you or the children and don't allow the dog to always win games.

Just say 'no'

Teach your child how to say a firm 'no' to the puppy if he does something unacceptable, such as nipping their fingers or chewing clothes. Explain that, for the puppy's own good, she should stop

playing with him immediately so that he realizes that any nipping or chewing will end the game and make life less fun. Drumming fingers on the floor to encourage the puppy to pounce on them will inevitably encourage him to try to gnaw at them. Ask your children to wave a toy for him to catch and chew instead.

It's a dog's world

Encouraging your children to learn about canine behaviour will help them to understand how dogs view the world. For instance, a dog can hear things that humans couldn't possibly pick up without specialist equipment. Often, when a dog appears to behave strangely, it can be a reaction to something he has heard and perceived to be dangerous, such as a distant thunderstorm.

Approaching a strange dog

1 The golden rule for approaching a strange dog is always to ask the owner first if you can stroke or pet him. The sweetest looking dogs can snap at a child, because of fear or a previous bad experience. Don't allow your child to approach a dog if the dog is over-excited or there are too many other children trying to stroke him. Don't allow your child to approach a dog if she has food on her skin or clothing, for example if she's just been eating an ice cream.

2 Observe the dog's body language. Does he look happy and confident or is he cowering behind his owner or looking hostile? If you are happy with the situation, and the owner gives permission, allow your child to approach the dog slowly. Remember that sudden actions can be perceived as frightening. During the approach, the child can hold out a hand slowly, palm down, and allow the dog to sniff.

No worries

Tell your children that, as much as possible, it's best to ignore a dog's fearful reactions if he is frightened by loud noises, even though it is tempting to pick him up and offer lots of cuddles. Unfortunately, if you do this you will confirm to the dog that there must be something for him to worry about and make him feel worse. See pages 118–119 for some tips on how you can help your dog to cope with nerves.

Good looking

Children should know that dogs tend to view staring by another dog as a confrontational act. Unfortunately, small children are often at a dog's eye-level height, and so it is important to train puppies from the beginning to accept eye contact with people. You can do this by getting down to the

3 If the dog seems receptive and wants to come closer, encourage your child to stroke him gently on the back of his head.

puppy's level regularly and spending time playing with him, talking to him, stroking his face and reassuring him so that he remains confident and finds this a positive, rewarding experience.

Safety first

Studies carried out in the USA reveal that dog bites are the second most common medical emergency, and smaller children are the most likely victims. If you have done your research thoroughly and chosen a breed with a reputation as a good family pet you will significantly decrease the risk of biting injury. However, any dog will bite if he is provoked sufficiently. Always supervise young children when they are around dogs and never leave them alone together. Discourage children from grabbing dogs around the neck and teach them how to approach a strange dog.

Question time

Q *Why do dogs wag their tails and growl at the same time?*
Because they are confused. Something – perhaps meeting a new dog – has aroused their suspicion, and they don't know whether to play or fight.

A Tail wagging can be a little like waving a white flag in a dangerous situation, and the growling is a verbal warning.

Q *Why do dogs lick each other? And why do they lick us? It tickles!*
Dogs lick each other in greeting. Young dogs tend to lick as a sign of submissiveness to older dogs. It is up to you whether you tolerate licking of humans, but it is not very hygienic.

A It's how a dog says hello. His mother licked him when he was born, to let him know her smell. It's not a good idea to let a dog lick you, as it could spread germs, and he should never lick your face. Say 'no' and give him a toy to lick instead. Always wash your hands if a dog licks you.

A puppy's needs
in his new home

Before you bring your puppy home, you will have to consider how you will supply all his physical needs. Every puppy requires good-quality dog food, fresh water, routine, exercise, companionship, shelter from the elements and a safe space to call his own. It is also a good idea to register with a vet before the puppy arrives and arrange an appointment for his first check-up.

Food

Puppies normally go to their new homes when they have been vaccinated, which is usually between seven and ten weeks old. This can be a stressful time for them, and any sudden dietary changes can result in gastric problems. To make the transition period easier, stock up on food that the breeder has recommended and offer this for the first week or two. Make changes to his diet very gradually to reduce the risk of gastric upsets.

Like babies, puppies grow at an incredibly rapid rate, and they require lots of calories. However, their stomachs are tiny, which is why you should offer several small meals throughout the day, rather than one or two large ones. In the early days your puppy will probably need up to four small feeds a day.

Buy the best quality dog food you can afford and meticulously follow the manufacturer's instructions as to how much and how often to feed. Pet-food manufacturers spend a fortune on researching the correct quantities and ingredients, so take advantage of their work rather than guessing that a couple of spoonfuls is about right.

Age-specific dog foods are available. If you have a puppy, choose a complete food designed to meet the nutritional needs of puppies. These

LEFT: Encourage your children to keep the puppy's water bowls filled with clean water.

OPPOSITE ABOVE: Meeting dogs is an important part of your puppy's training. As an adult, he will have to interact with people and other dogs, and socialization classes are a good way of learning how to do this.

OPPOSITE BELOW: Never allow your children to feed the puppy chocolate, which is poisonous to dogs and can even be fatal.

are available as wet or dry formulations. You should continue to offer this food for the first year before moving to adult dog food.

Drink up!
Access to fresh clean water is vital. Place more than one bowl of water around the house and encourage your children to fill the bowls daily.

A place of his own
He also needs a safe area – a bed or crate – to which he can retreat. Teach your children to understand that the puppy is not a toy and to respect his personal space and recognize this place as a no-go area (see pages 40–41).

Health
The puppy's first check-up at the veterinary surgery is an ideal time to chat to the vet about worming, flea and parasite treatments, microchipping and vaccinations (see pages 44–45 and 99–101).

Social work
Ask your veterinary surgery whether they run any puppy socialization classes. If they do, register your puppy. This is a great way for him and your family to meet other puppies and owners. By signing your puppy up for a class, you can make a good start on helping him cope with family life and grow into a confident adult dog.

Keeping your dog
happy and healthy

Most families are keen to do as much as they possibly can to look after their dog, but some of these efforts may have an unwanted effect. Explain to the children before the dog's arrival that any form of physical punishment or cruel treatment will have a negative impact on the dog, but also that sometimes, over a lengthy period, too much kindness can be equally distressing.

Pampered pooches

In today's celebrity-conscious world, people sometimes want to emulate those socialites who seem to view dogs, particularly toy dogs, as living fashion accessories. Designer fashion houses have waiting lists for their doggy bags, which are basically hold-alls used to carry and show off these cute little canines. The trend for carrying puppies and small dogs, rather than allowing them to walk on their own four paws, is now increasingly evident. However, animal welfare societies warn against the practice of carrying dogs everywhere, pointing out that it can be distressing for the animal and that regular opportunities for walking are essential to keep a dog's limbs strong and healthy. There is also a danger that highly strung dogs may find the experience of being taken to loud parties very upsetting, particularly if there is strobe lighting or flash photography.

Sheltered lives

Dogs need plenty of exercise and bigger, more energetic breeds need lots of access to the outside world. However, all dogs need to be able to shelter from extremes of weather, and that includes heat as well as cold. Dogs are unable to perspire in the same way as humans and can quickly become over-heated. The sun can turn a parked vehicle into an oven in a short space of time, so leaving your dog in your car while you do the shopping is very dangerous.

Some hardy breeds can happily live outdoors, provided they have access to a warm, draught-free shelter with a comfortable bed and sufficient food and water. However, older dogs and those with thin coats, such as a Greyhound or Lurcher,

Do!

- Provide your dog with appropriate veterinary treatment
- Establish routines for meals and exercise sessions
- Create opportunities for learning and having fun
- Give shelter from the elements
- Carry out a socialization programme

Don't!

- Shout at or hit your dog
- Leave him alone so he becomes bored
- Isolate him from the family
- Allow him to become fat
- Carry him everywhere and treat him like a baby

will not be happy staying permanently outdoors and should have their space in the home.

Not a toy

Just because a puppy is small, or a certain breed is classed as a toy dog, it doesn't mean that they are not real dogs. Children must learn to appreciate that such dogs are not toys and should not be carried around like dolls. Encouraging children and dogs to have fun together in ways that allow the dog to engage in normal canine behaviour will ensure that everyone remains happy. Even tiny dogs, such as a Chihuahua or Bichon Frise, can enjoy learning basic obedience and doing tricks. They may even be suitable for a sport such as agility.

ABOVE: Your dog needs affection to thrive, but warn your children that he has to be allowed his own space, too.

LEFT: Hardy breeds, such as Huskies and Border Collies, will be content living outdoors, so long as they are fit and young and have a suitable shelter.

OPPOSITE: Regular use of doggy bags to carry your puppy is not recommended. Dogs need plenty of exercise to stay healthy.

Lessons in tolerance
for children and dogs

Some family pets are tolerant of children and will stalwartly endure all kinds of indignities, from being dressed up in baby clothes to sitting in the back of little trailers and being taken for rides around the neighbourhood. However, it is important for children to grasp the concept of respect and not to force any dog to do something that he obviously does not enjoy.

Watch out!

All dogs, no matter how placid they may be, have their breaking point, and children who don't recognize the warning signals can get bitten. Learning to see the world as dogs do and to look for and react to warning signals will help reduce the risk. The signs of canine fear or potential aggression can include:

- Wagging the tail in wide, slow sweeps accompanied by growling
- Ears straight up
- Lips lifted back to reveal teeth
- Hackles raised
- Dilated, enlarged pupils
- Showing the whites of the eyes (when not normally visible)

Question time

Q *I don't think the dog likes me any more. He used to be really cuddly, but now he's just grumpy and growls when I want to give him a hug. Why does he hate me now? Dogs don't suddenly start to hate the people they have previously loved. They could become frightened of them, but if you have not been deliberately cruel to him it can be difficult to know exactly why his attitude towards you has changed.*

A Sometimes, when dogs grow older, they don't like as much hugging and handling as they used to do. This may be because their joints and bones are older and more painful, so hugs and cuddles from you may actually be hurting them. The dog can't tell you when something hurts him, so he tries to let you know by using other body language, such as growling, biting, trembling or even hiding from you so that you can't find him. We can take him to the vet to see if there is anything physically wrong that might explain his behaviour. In the meantime, just be patient and kind, and let the dog come to you for attention rather than the other way round.

LEFT: When you are selecting a family pet, choose a breed that will be happy to be cuddled by children.

OPPOSITE: Your child can use treats to help socialize the puppy to any actions, such as putting up an umbrella, that he may dislike.

Coping strategies

As soon as your puppy arrives, embark on a socialization programme to help him cope with all the different things he may encounter as a family pet (see pages 48–49).

Ideally, the breeder will already have made him familiar with household items, such as the television, radio and vacuum cleaner, and accustomed him to meeting various people. However, don't assume that he is confident with everything and try to introduce him to as many new sights and sounds as possible. Always reward calm behaviour and try to ignore any negative reactions as much as possible.

If your dog appears worried by something – the sight of an umbrella being put up, for example – you can encourage your children to help by breaking the movement down into small sections and rewarding the dog with a treat for tolerating each movement. It can be a good lesson for children to learn how to make a dog more confident and to appreciate the importance of patience.

Child's-eye view
'I'd like my dog to do a cartwheel or a roly-poly.' Nicole, age 5

Tip to parents
Children have little concept of a dog's physical limitations, and in the world of cartoons, films and books dogs are often portrayed performing human feats. Explain to your child that dogs can't do everything and encourage her to focus on teaching tricks the dog can do, such as a roll over or high five (see pages 86–89).

chapter 3

The first few days

Now that you and your family have talked through the responsibilities of dog ownership, done your research into the different breeds and decided which puppy you are going to buy, you need to prepare your house for the big day. This chapter will help you get your home ready, buy everything that is required and cope with those all-important first days. Start by stocking up on doggy equipment.

Collar and lead

There is an enormous range of bright, funky designs to appeal to children, but fit and comfort are the most important factors when it comes to choosing a collar. Puppies grow quickly, so don't spend a fortune and buy the best. You can buy a better quality collar once the dog is fully grown.

Have an identity disc engraved with the dog's name and a contact number, and attach this to the collar.

Food and bowls

The best bowls have wide bases and are heavy enough not to tip over. Puppies can chew plastic, so a better choice may be ceramic or metal. A portable, folding water bowl is useful when you are travelling.

Stock up on the food that is recommended by the breeder (see pages 26–27) and store it in a container with a strong lid.

Poop scoops

You can buy eco-friendly paper bags or plastic nappy sacks to pick up dog faeces. Dispose of them in dog-waste bins or with the household rubbish.

Bed and bedding

In the early days, a strong cardboard box with a section cut out for the puppy to climb in through is ideal and can be easily replaced if the puppy decides to start chewing. Remove any metal staples on the box that the dog could swallow. Place the bed in a quiet corner of his safe room (see page 34) and teach your children to respect this as the puppy's space, which they should leave well alone. Stock up on replacement boxes in case of accidents and line the box with newspaper and a warm blanket or invest in a specially designed, washable dog bed or beanbag. Charity shops and thrift stores are good sources of inexpensive towels and blankets.

Grooming kit

Different brushes and combs are available, depending on whether your puppy is a long- or wire-haired breed. Combs with the finest tines are for removing fleas. Stock up on dog shampoo (human shampoos often contain chemicals that will irritate his skin) and keep old towels for drying him after bathing. You will also need dog toothpaste and a dog toothbrush. (See page 52 for more on grooming kit.)

Clicker

This small, plastic device makes a clicking noise when pressed and is used for training. The earlier you start training the better (see pages 76–77). It's a good idea to buy several clickers so that you always have one available.

Toys

Invest in a few toys that your dog can safely chew or play with. Non-toxic materials, such as rubber, are best. Buy toys that are suitable for your puppy's size of mouth.

Creating a
dog-proof
zone

Once you have done your shopping, the next step in your preparations is to make your home as dog-proof as possible. This can be fun for children, who can help you locate potential dangers and spots where little puppies could easily squeeze in and find themselves trapped. Different areas, such as the kitchen, living room and garden, all harbour hidden dangers.

Be safe

Make one room in the house as secure as you possibly can and keep the puppy enclosed there when he first arrives. You can gradually introduce him to other areas of the home as the days go by.

You might want to think about installing a child's stair-gate so that you can block off the puppy's safe room. Later, you can use the gate to keep the puppy off stairways or out of areas you don't want him to go. You may be able to find a second-hand stair-gate in a charity shop.

Kitchens, which are full of appliances like washing machines and dishwashers, are particularly dangerous places for a curious puppy, who may decide to climb inside the washing machine for a quiet nap, unbeknown to

Question time

Q *What's the best way to pick up the puppy and take him home?*
You will need to arrange a collection date with the breeder. Try to arrive in good time, so that everyone is relaxed. Although your children might want to hold the puppy, it is better to transport him in a secure travelling box. Take an old sweater or blanket to the breeder a few days beforehand and ask for this to be put into the puppy's bed. When you pick up the puppy, put the sweater in his travelling box and later in his bed.

A We will have to arrange a time with the breeder and make sure we arrive good and early so that we're all as calm as possible, even though we'll all be really excited. I know you will want to hold the puppy, but we need a proper box to bring him home in. He will feel much better in his box than if he is squeezed in your arms throughout the entire journey. So that he can get used to his new home, we can ask the breeder to put one of your old sweaters in the puppy's bed for a few days before we pick him up. When we get home we can put it in his bed to remind him of his doggy family, so he won't be worried about being in a new place.

ABOVE: The best way to bring your puppy home is in a secure travelling box, ideally lined with an old sweater that was placed for a few days in the puppy's bed at the breeder's.

OPPOSITE: A child's stair-gate is ideal for preventing your puppy from entering certain areas of the house.

someone who switches on the machine. If there are any gaps under the kitchen units, erect temporary boards until the puppy has grown too big to squeeze underneath.

Check living rooms for dangers such as dangling wires behind electrical equipment, low coffee tables from which a puppy could pull down items, such as cups of hot coffee, and fragile ornaments within paw-reach. Clear up anything that you don't want chewed. If necessary, buy some extra toy boxes with lids, so that children can tidy their toys safely away.

Ask the children to create notices, such as 'Check for the puppy', which can be pinned on to the front and back doors. These may help everyone remember to shut the doors and prevent the puppy from escaping. If there is a cat flap, make sure it is locked when the puppy is around.

Tip to parents
You will already have scheduled the date for the puppy's arrival and your children might enjoy making and decorating a countdown calendar, which they can mark off in anticipation of the big day.

Welcome home
to your new puppy!

Resolve to make your puppy's first few hours and days in his new home as calm and pleasant as possible. This will not always be easy when you have excitable children who are desperate to hold and cuddle him all the time and then start arguing about whose turn it is. It is important to explain to children how frightening their behaviour can be to a little puppy.

Preparing the ground

If you discuss beforehand how the puppy might be feeling when he arrives, your children will have a better idea about how they should behave while he is settling into the home. Things to ask your children to consider can include:

- How do you think the puppy will feel when he gets here? Will he be happy, sad or frightened?
- What sort of things might we do that could scare a puppy?
- Will he be missing his mum and his brothers and sisters?
- How can we welcome him and make him feel more confident?
- Who is going to hold the puppy first?
- How long will you hold the puppy before it is someone else's turn?
- Do you think puppies get tired easily?

Child's-eye view
'I think on the first day my puppy will be so excited he won't be able to sleep.' Maisie, age 3

Tip to parents
Children often assume that animals will feel the same emotions as them. Try to explain that the puppy may well be excited, but that he will also be a little overwhelmed by all the noise and confusion and will need lots of naps and quiet time.

- How will we know if the puppy is tired?
- We need to teach the puppy to toilet outdoors, so how are we going to do that and how can you help?
- How can we introduce him to all our other pets?
- Which room is he going to stay in for the first few days?
- What are our house rules going to be for the puppy?

Introductions

If you have other pets, such as another dog or a cat, take time to introduce them slowly and safely. You can put the puppy in a crate and allow the other pet to sniff him. Alternatively, let them meet on neutral territory, with both dogs on leads. Make lots of fuss of the existing pet so that he doesn't lose confidence or become jealous and try to maintain his food and exercise routine as much as possible to reassure him that all is well.

ABOVE: Supervise the puppy as he meets your other pets.

BELOW: Ask children to approach the new puppy with respect.

OPPOSITE: Children can help with house-training by taking the dog out to toilet after a meal.

Question time

Q *Why does my puppy wee everywhere?*
You must expect some accidents, particularly at first when the puppy is getting used to new scents and sounds and has not yet settled into a routine. Little puppies have small bladders and cannot hold water for very long. The more you show your puppy when and where he should go to the toilet, the quicker he will learn.

A It's because he's little and doesn't know where he is supposed to go. It's up to us to teach him. We must keep taking him outside when he needs the toilet, especially after he has just woken up or been fed. When he does go where he is supposed to, don't forget to let him know by telling him what a good boy he is.

Lifting and carrying
a puppy

A puppy who is happy to be lifted and carried is much easier to handle when he grows up. Learning the correct way to lift and carry a dog is essential for building confidence in both puppy and the child. The puppy will want to feel secure and comfortable in your child's arms, and you must judge whether you think your child is capable of holding him securely.

Lifting and carrying a puppy

1 Your child should crouch down and bend his knees, keeping his back straight so he doesn't injure himself when he lifts. He should gather the puppy firmly to him, with one arm around the dog's chest to stop him escaping and the other arm under the puppy's bottom for support. Encourage your child to talk gently to the dog to instil confidence and trust.

2 The puppy should be kept close to his body as the child slowly straightens to an upright position, keeping his back straight, so that the dog feels safe and doesn't jump from his arms. If the puppy feels in danger of being dropped, he will struggle to free himself, so it's important to maintain a secure, but not tight, hold and to keep talking reassuringly.

Dogs aren't toys

Carrying a puppy needs care, thought and a degree of coordination, so it's unwise to let small children lift and carry puppies without proper supervision. Young children aged about six and under have a short attention span (and the younger they are, the shorter it is), so they soon forget not to hug tightly or run with the dog, or they may drop the puppy when they have finished playing with him, as they would a toy.

If such rough handling goes unchecked, the dog will become wary of being picked up and may show aggression and/or fear when someone approaches. What's more, a puppy's bones are delicate and will not develop fully until the dog is a few months old. If your child yanks or pulls him, he could sustain injuries that will have serious consequences later in life.

Why puppies wriggle

The majority of dogs don't particularly like being picked up and carried, and they will respond by wriggling when people try to do so. This is because dogs feel vulnerable without the use of their legs to run away from danger or defend themselves. If a dog is held firmly or squeezed, his instincts will tell him that he is under threat, and he will naturally try to escape or fight off a perceived attacker. Help your child understand why his puppy struggles and objects when he tries to pick him up or holds him too tightly, so that he doesn't assume that the dog simply doesn't like him.

3 When walking with the puppy, your child should carry the dog close to his chest and be alert for any signs of him tensing up in readiness to try to jump down. To put the puppy down, simply reverse the actions.

Do! encourage your child to …
- Support the puppy's bottom
- Hold the dog securely to prevent him jumping free
- Talk calmly and reassuringly
- Take things slowly

Don't! encourage your child to …
- Hug or squeeze the puppy
- Shout excitedly while holding the dog
- Pick up a dog that's too big
- Move abruptly or run when holding a puppy

Too much
smother
love

All puppies need to sleep a lot, particularly during the day, as this is when they recharge their energy levels and get on with the business of growing. Unfortunately, in a household of lively children it is not always easy to ensure that a young puppy is left alone to enjoy his naps. Make it a golden rule that children should never be allowed to wake the puppy when he is sleeping.

ABOVE: To discourage puppies from developing bad habits, such as tail chasing and play biting, allow them to expend any excess energy on a vigorous game with a favourite toy.

OPPOSITE: Puppies need their beauty sleep. Ask your children not to disturb the puppy when he is having a nap, even if this is in the middle of the day.

Let sleeping dogs lie

Ask your children to consider how scared they would feel if they were suddenly or roughly pulled from their beds when they were fast asleep. A tiny puppy will find such an experience just as intimidating and would not be happy to play with them.

When the puppy does wake up, make sure that he has some time when he is not being handled so that he can safely explore his environment and become familiar with the sights and sounds of his new home.

Down time

Just like children, some puppies can become a little over-excited or irritable if they have not had enough sleep. If you think this is happening, it's best to

Tip to parents

Discourage your children from touching the dog when he is sleeping, eating or chewing a rawhide bone. Even though your dog may tolerate this type of treatment, other dogs may not, and your child will be vulnerable to being bitten.

give him a little time-out from all the stimulation in the home. Do this by putting him in his bed or an indoor crate where he can experience some quiet time and calm down.

Never scold or be heavy-handed with the puppy when you want him to calm down and be quiet or he will come to perceive being put in his bed or crate as a negative experience. Simply pick him up gently and put him down on his bed – the puppy should soon close his eyes and fall asleep. Always allow your puppy some quiet time after he has eaten so that he is able to digest his food.

Play time

As you get to know your puppy it will quickly become clear when he is likely to be more active. Usually this is in the evenings, although he may well have a 'mad half hour' during the day when he tears around, chasing his tail or play-biting. Rather than allowing him to develop bad habits, use these active periods to channel his energy more positively. If possible, start to engage him in play a few minutes before he has a manic moment and introduce games, such as retrieving a toy or playing hide-and-seek with some titbits. By having a lively game with him or taking him for a walk before bedtime, you will help him to sleep well. His pre-bedtime walk is also essential to help him become house-trained.

Keeping
the peace

Teaching your children to be gentle and to overcome their feelings of frustration if a puppy doesn't immediately respond to them is an important life lesson. They need to learn to respect the dog, but, at the same time, it's essential that the presence of the new puppy, who will inevitably be the centre of attention for a few days or weeks, doesn't make a child feel neglected.

Sibling rivalry

All children are unique in their behaviour, and even siblings brought up in the same household can surprise you with the way they react to a new dog in the family. Sometimes a child may become slightly jealous, perhaps if a puppy consistently obeys commands better for another family member. If this happens, try to explain that the puppy is not doing anything on purpose and is not deliberately ignoring her.

You can also help by supervising some quality time between the child and the dog. Give the child some special treats for the dog that can be used in training, and try to teach her how to use clearer commands and signals, so that the puppy learns to come to all members of the family on command or go from a standing position into a sit (see pages 78–81). If you emphasize

Question time

Q *My son is four years old and can sometimes be a little rough with the puppy. How can I stop this?*
If you have a very small child, under the age of six, sit him down comfortably with the puppy and then guide his hands so that he can learn how to stroke and hold the animal. The golden rule should always be 'gently does it'. Equally, discourage the puppy from becoming over-boisterous and engaging in undesirable behaviour, such as nipping the child's ankles or fingers. It may be cute in a tiny puppy, but it's less so when the dog is fully grown. Teach your child to say the word 'no' and immediately end the game, so that the puppy learns it is much more fun when he plays gently. Equally, stop your child from playing with the puppy if he becomes rough.

A Remember that you must always be gentle with the puppy or he will become frightened and won't want to play with you at all. Let me hold your hand while you stroke him. You can feel how softly we are doing this. If it's any rougher than this, the game will have to end.

Tip to parents

Avoid arguments about whose turn it is to hold a puppy by investing in an egg-timer or setting the microwave to beep after five or ten minutes. Children get very upset if they suspect another child is 'getting more time'. Using a timer will appeal to their sense of fair play and provide an opportunity for the puppy to be put into his bed for quiet time.

the importance of using reward and positive motivation when training, the child should soon enjoy successful results.

No hitting

If a child accidentally or purposefully hits the puppy, the animal will soon lose confidence and be extremely wary of interacting with the child in the future. For this reason, the importance of supervision, particularly with young children whose movements are less coordinated, cannot be over-emphasized.

Space invaders

Teach children not to disturb the puppy when he is eating. Ask them to imagine how they would feel if they were just about to sit down to a lovely lunch and someone came up behind them and lifted them right out of their chair. Clearly, this would be irritating, to say the least, and the same applies to your puppy. No matter how good-natured he is, it is important for children to respect his privacy and allow him to eat undisturbed. If a dog is taken away from his food before he has finished he may begin to develop guarding behaviour. Left unchecked, this could be dangerous as the dog could start to snap.

ABOVE: If your child has difficulty in getting the dog to obey commands, try giving her some high-value treats (such as pieces of chicken) to use during training.

RIGHT: Make sure each member of the family is giving the dog the same signals and verbal commands for the same actions. If you use different commands, he may become confused.

OPPOSITE: A small child should be shown how to hold and stroke a puppy gently.

Going to
the vet

As soon as possible after picking up your puppy you should arrange for him to visit the vet for a health check. Even if you think the puppy is in good health, it is useful for the vet to give him the all clear, otherwise some congenital or hereditary problems may go undetected and cause problems in later life.

First visit

Make the first visit as positive an experience as possible for your puppy, using treats and toys before, during and after the occasion. Transport him in his carrier and leave plenty of time to arrive for the appointment early, so that he has a chance to sit in the waiting room and get used to the sights and smells associated with the surgery. Taking the puppy early will also provide an opportunity for staff members to meet him, and he will enjoy plenty of attention from everyone so that he begins to build positive associations with the surgery.

Most vets don't mind one or two children being involved in the consultation, but if you have a large family this could be problematic as most consulting rooms are quite small. If you're in doubt, phone the surgery beforehand.

Your vet will chat with you first to find out whether the puppy has been wormed and vaccinated (see pages 99–101), what his diet is and so on. You may also be asked about any pre-breeding tests that were carried out on his parents. All this information should have been provided to you by the breeder.

Examining the puppy

For a full clinical examination, you will lift the puppy on to the examination table and hold him steady while the vet looks him over (see right for the different checks that will be made).

If necessary, your vet will prescribe medication against fleas and other parasites, and discuss when you will need to return for vaccinations against viral diseases. You will also get advice on the importance of maintaining regular dental care, neutering, microchipping and any puppy socialization classes that are held at the clinic.

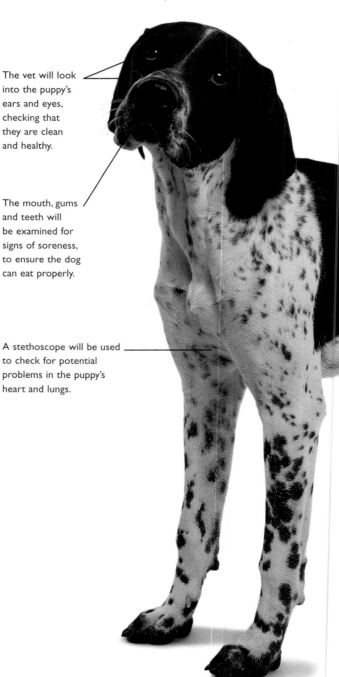

The vet will look into the puppy's ears and eyes, checking that they are clean and healthy.

The mouth, gums and teeth will be examined for signs of soreness, to ensure the dog can eat properly.

A stethoscope will be used to check for potential problems in the puppy's heart and lungs.

Q *Isn't the vet being mean and hurting my puppy by sticking a needle in him?*
You can explain that there's no need to be concerned as the needles used to vaccinate puppies are small and fine and that the shots are given in the scruff of the neck where the skin is quite thick. Vets love animals and everything they do is done to help them.

A There's honestly no need to worry that the vet is going to hurt the puppy. The needles are so small and fine that the puppy will hardly feel anything at all. The shots are given into the back of the dog's neck (known as the scruff) because this is where the skin is quite thick. You can always help to cheer up the dog afterwards by giving him a special treat and cuddling him.

The vet will look at the coat to determine if there is evidence of flea infestation, which can be common in puppies.

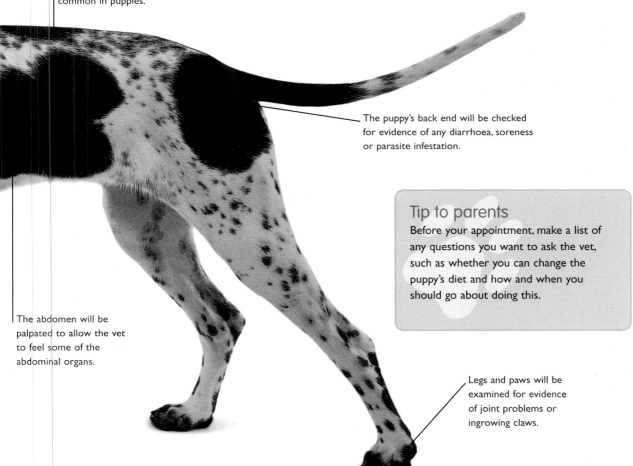

The puppy's back end will be checked for evidence of any diarrhoea, soreness or parasite infestation.

Tip to parents

Before your appointment, make a list of any questions you want to ask the vet, such as whether you can change the puppy's diet and how and when you should go about doing this.

The abdomen will be palpated to allow the vet to feel some of the abdominal organs.

Legs and paws will be examined for evidence of joint problems or ingrowing claws.

chapter 4

Routine matters

The quicker you can get your puppy into a routine, the quicker he will settle down. It's important that the whole family works together to help the puppy to get used to his new home. This chapter looks at the main areas in which children can take responsibility for their new pet, from feeding and grooming to helping the puppy fit into his surroundings.

Importance of routine

Puppies are creatures of habit and this can be used to good effect in their training and in helping them settle in quickly. Taking him to the same spot in your garden to toilet, for example, will help him learn where you want him to perform, and scheduling toilet trips at the same times, after meals and before bed, will reinforce the message. Don't expect house-training to be achieved immediately, however; it takes time (see pages 114–115 for information about toilet problems).

Dinner time

Establish a dinner-time routine, giving meals at the same time every day, and make sure that play sessions take place after the puppy has eaten. Adopt the same regime as your breeder in the early days: if your puppy is used to four meals a day, continue with this for at least a week or so, before starting a new routine. Puppies are clever and will soon start letting you know if you are late with something. Standing with a food bowl in their mouth is enough of a reminder for most people.

If you have allocated the responsibility for feeding the puppy to your children, it is important to supervise them and make sure that the task is done properly. Help them understand how important it is by asking them to imagine how they would feel if one day mum or dad forgot to give them their breakfast until lunchtime and then woke them up from a sleep to give them their supper or, worse still, forgot to feed them at all. (See pages 50–51 for how your child can be involved in feeding the dog.)

Bedtime

As a parent or guardian you will know the importance of a regular, night-time routine to help children calm down and fall asleep easily. It is just as important to do this with a puppy, although the technique is slightly different.

Rather than giving the puppy a bath and a bedtime story, you should start the night-time routine by putting a stop to boisterous games half an hour before you want the puppy to settle down. Take him for a walk, let him go to the toilet and give him a quiet cuddle. His eyes will begin to close quite quickly as he relaxes, and you can gently put him into his bed. Keeping his bed in a quiet, warm room will stop him being disturbed by other family activities and noise.

New sights
and sounds

What if your kids never left the house? If they never played with friends or met new people? What if the only people they knew were family? When they did eventually come across strangers they would be wary and fearful. This is what it's like for a new puppy. Coming into a home with all its noises and different creatures can be scary.

About the house

It's important to make the puppy comfortable with the key sights and sounds around the house. Sit down with your child and work out a list of things the puppy should gradually be exposed to. The list might include very regular things such as different rooms, the television, telephone, your child's toys; but don't forget more unusual sounds, such as computer games, the washing machine and the vacuum cleaner.

LEFT AND ABOVE: A home is full of strange noises. Be sure your pooch is familiar with day-to-day sounds in different areas of the house.

OPPOSITE: Take every opportunity to introduce your dog to people who visit your home. It's important to get him used to regular visitors, such as friends, postmen or delivery men.

Visitors

If your dog hasn't had all his jabs, don't delay in socialization. Invite regular visitors, relatives and particularly your children's friends. Your kids can take an active role in showing their friends how to behave with a new puppy. Remember that children can be boisterous when they're together, so keep an eye on them. Make sure all new meetings happen close to the dog's basket as this will provide some comforting odours that will relax him.

The dog about town

Socializing a dog is a great project for a child and you can take one thing from your list to do each day of, say, a school holiday, ticking it off on successful completion. Once the dog is fully inoculated, walkies open up a world of new experiences and your children will love showing off the puppy to strangers. Here are some of the people, places and things your dog should meet and greet when out on a walk:

Different people
- [ ] A mixture of ages
- [ ] People walking other dogs
- [ ] Delivery men
- [ ] People wearing crash helmets or carrying walking sticks and umbrellas
- [ ] Joggers
- [ ] Men with beards/people with glasses

Other animals
- [ ] Other dogs
- [ ] Cats
- [ ] Livestock (cattle, pigs, sheep)
- [ ] Horses

Vehicles
- [ ] Cars
- [ ] Bicycles
- [ ] Motorbikes
- [ ] Buses
- [ ] Lorries

Environments
- [ ] Friends' houses
- [ ] Shopping centres
- [ ] Playgroups
- [ ] Parks
- [ ] Obedience classes
- [ ] School yard
- [ ] Countryside

Question time

Q *Why does my dog always wee on posts?* *This is a common question as it is a behaviour pattern that is so foreign to a child's sensibilities. It's a dog's instinct to mark his territory through urine and to 'overmark' other dogs' scent trails.*

A He does it because he's marking his territory. He's leaving a calling card to tell other dogs who he is, that he's a boy and that he lives in this area. See how he sniffed the post first. What's probably happened is that another dog has marked it first and now Charlie is overmarking.

Q *Why does he smell other dogs' bottoms?* *This is another behaviour pattern that will be alien to your child. The olfactory system of dogs is their primary means of investigation. They can learn many things from one sniff when greeting a fellow canine, including the other dog's general health and if a female pooch is sexually healthy. A dog's anal glands are also located here and carry the dog's individual scent.*

A Sniffing is a dog's way of saying hello and finding out about another dog. There's more to it than just sniffing though. Look how they bump each other first. They're finding out who's the bigger and who will be the boss. It sets the rules for the play that will follow.

Child's-eye view
'I think a puppy might be scared at night, when it's dark, because he's missing his mum.' Lily, age 7

Tip to parents
Putting a blanket that smells of his mother in the puppy's basket will help comfort him at night.

Getting some food for thought

Puppies are usually introduced to solid food when they are about three weeks old. By the time you get your dog, usually between seven and ten weeks old, he will be eating four small meals a day. You can gradually reduce this to three by about 12 weeks of age and then two feeds at four or five months old. Adult dogs need one or two meals a day, which can be moist or dry.

All change

When you first get your puppy, it is advisable to feed him on the same food that the breeder has been offering. Stock up on supplies before you bring the puppy home and maintain the diet for the first few weeks. After that time, make any changes very gradually to avoid the risk of gastric upset. In addition, ensure your dog has fresh water at all times.

Balanced diet

Dry 'complete' dog foods are designed to provide a nutritionally balanced diet. However, some foods may not be nutritionally complete and may require additional supplements. Check the labelling to find out what the food provides. A diet composed solely of moist foods may also require dry supplements in order to keep your dog's teeth in good order; dry foods are good for oral health as they are abrasive on the teeth when eaten. Ask your vet for advice if you have any concerns about feeding.

Greedy guts

Dogs can be greedy and will eat just about anything, whether it is good for them or not. In addition, children are often guilty of feeding titbits from the table, particularly things they are not keen on eating themselves. This encourages begging and will add extra calories to the puppy's diet. If you occasionally give the dog a special treat, feed him after your own meal and serve it directly into his dish.

Can I help?

Involve your children in the dog's feeding regime to help them develop a sense of responsibility and to allow the dog to build positive associations. If the children take it in turns to present the dog food in a dish, they will become popular. Very young children can help by fetching the dish or spooning food into it, although you should always keep an eye on how much they put in the dish.

Manners!

It is dangerous for dogs to snatch food, particularly from children, so teach your dog to be patient and to wait for permission. This also reinforces the concept that he is not the leader of the pack and that children must be respected. You should supervise feeding times.

Question time

Q *Urgh! Why does my dog keep on passing wind?*
It could be because you are feeding him too many titbits. Foods containing sugar, salt or garlic can all have this effect. Stick to a complete dog food and only feed healthy snacks, such as rawhide chews or carrot sticks. If the problem continues you should seek veterinary advice.

A He's probably having difficulty digesting his food. Some dogs have problems if they eat too many titbits or human food. From now on, let's try to feed him nothing but his dog food and a few healthy treats to see if that helps.

Q *Why does my dog sometimes eat grass and make himself sick?*
No one really understands why dogs do this, although one theory is that the dog is seeking extra roughage. As you have observed, grass is a natural emetic, so to avoid a mess indoors keep him outside until he has been sick. If you are worried, check with your vet.

A Lots of dogs do this. If the dog has eaten something that's made him feel poorly he might eat the grass to help him throw up and get rid of it.

Feeding your dog

1 With the bowl of food in one hand, your child should approach the dog and ask him to sit. She should then crouch down and put a hand on the dog's collar before placing the bowl a little distance in front of him.

2 The child should give the 'wait' command (see pages 80–81), putting the dog back into a sit if he breaks into a stand.

3 When the dog has relaxed into a sit and made eye contact with the child, it is time to give a release command, such as 'get it', so that the dog can eat the food. Getting the food is his reward for showing self-control.

A puppy's
big
brush off

Grooming should be a fun experience for your puppy and something everyone enjoys doing for him. Try to groom him every day so that he gets used to being handled. Demonstrate to your children how to be gentle, particularly if you have a long-haired dog, and if necessary remind them of the fuss they make having the tangles removed from their own hair.

Can I help?

Small children will have difficulty controlling a wriggling puppy and managing a brush at the same time. Don't let your child groom her dog unsupervised; an older child or adult should hold the puppy while the younger child gently brushes him. Make sure children wash their hands carefully after grooming.

If a child thinks she has found a flea while grooming the dog, she should first check what it is with an adult. You can tell it's a flea, rather than just a speck of dirt, because flea dirt contains congealed blood and will dilute to a pinkish colour if you put it on a piece of damp cotton wool. Remove the flea from the flea comb with a paper towel and dispose of it in the household rubbish (see pages 100–101 for more on removing fleas).

Make grooming sessions short, giving lots of verbal praise, and follow it up with a treat or a game for the puppy so he thinks that grooming is enjoyable. Getting your dog used to being picked up and put on a table to be groomed will help him cope when he visits the vet.

Essential kit

Your dog's coat type will determine the equipment you need, but you will need some, if not all, of the following:

- **Slicker brush** Great for removing dead hair and debris from dense, short coats or curly coats, but if used roughly it can pull and irritate the skin.
- **Bristle and pin brush** Ideal for most short-haired breeds.
- **Grooming mitts** These can be used to help remove dead hair and dirt and to polish the coat.
- **Steel comb and flea comb** These will remove tangles, fleas and ticks.
- **Cotton wool** Useful for cleaning the dog's eyes. Work gently, always wiping outwards, and use separate damp pads for each eye.
- **Scissors** If you don't take your dog to a professional dog groomer, scissors may be required for occasional hair trimming. Always use sharp, good-quality scissors with round ends so that you don't accidentally nick his skin.
- **Nail clippers** Use clippers only if you can do the job properly; ask your vet to demonstrate first.
- **Dog toothbrush and dog toothpaste** See pages 56–57 for a guide to cleaning your dog's teeth.

Grooming

1 Before your child begins grooming, put down an old blanket or towel or some newspapers for the puppy to stand on, and take off his collar.

2 The child should begin by brushing with long, smooth strokes from head to tail, combing out any matted fur. You should cut out any mats with scissors if necessary. She can use a flea comb to check for fleas or ticks.

Question time

Q *Why does my dog smell so bad?*
Some dogs are better than others at cleaning themselves, and you may have to resort to regular bathing and to keeping the coat clipped. An older dog may have developed stiff joints or back pain that makes it difficult for him to clean himself. Bitches are more likely than dogs to get urine on the hair. Clipping

around this area may help. There could be medical reasons, including a discharge from the anal glands, so have him checked by a vet.

A Now that he's getting a bit older he can't clean himself as well has he used to do. Perhaps we need to help by clipping his coat. Let's ask the vet for his advice.

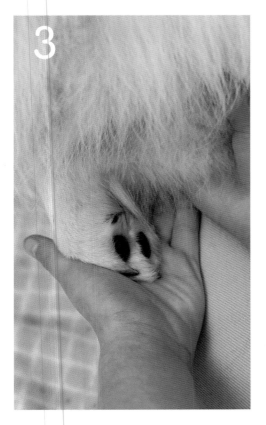

3 Encourage your child to examine the puppy's feet to check for cuts or gravel in his pads.

4 If necessary, you or your child can gently wipe the eyes clean. You should check the puppy's ears and if necessary clean them gently with damp cotton wool pads. Finally, put on the puppy's collar and give him a hug and a treat.

Time for a bath
and some fun!

Just like children, some dogs take special delight in getting themselves as dirty as possible when they're out playing. Even if you don't show your dog it will be necessary to bathe him occasionally, and if he suffers from a skin allergy or develops fleas your vet may prescribe a special shampoo. Bathing helps remove dead hair and debris from the coat, making the puppy smell a lot fresher.

Soap stars

There is a huge range of canine shampoos, for different breeds and coat types and colours. Puppies need a mild puppy shampoo that will not irritate their skin. Don't use human shampoo or washing-up liquid on your dog, as these may irritate his skin or contain chemicals that could be toxic if he licks his coat. You can also buy coat conditioners to apply after the shampoo and make your dog's coat soft and shiny, but rinse these out properly with warm, clean water.

Professional dog groomers have hairdryers on stands that circulate air over the dog while he is in a cage. However, an ordinary hairdryer will do the job just as well, as long as it has heat controls so that you can select the coolest setting.

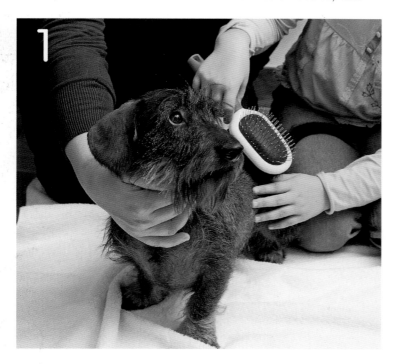

Bathing your dog 1 Fill the bath with warm, tepid water, testing with an elbow just as you would for a baby. Put down towels for the dog to stand on and have towels ready to dry him with. Your child can help by brushing the dog thoroughly to remove as many dead hairs as possible.

2 Gently lift the dog into the water. Use a jug to pour water on his coat, being careful not to get water in his eyes or ears.

How often?

Bathe your dog as often as he needs it, but generally not more than once a month. Bathing too often removes the natural oils from his coat, and these are needed to keep him warm and dry. Older dogs and those with thinner coats should be bathed less often than young, boisterous dogs or those with thick, dense coats.

Can I help?

If the weather is hot, it can be fun to bathe the dog outside. Children love hosing off the dog, but always supervise this to make sure that no water goes into the dog's eyes or ears. In colder weather, you will have to bathe the dog indoors, either in the sink, using a hose attachment, or in the bath. You will probably need to restrain the dog yourself during bathing (putting a non-slip mat on the bottom of the bath will help the dog to grip and make him easier to handle), but your child can help with the preliminary brushing and drying afterwards.

Tip to parents
Dogs love to shake themselves vigorously after they have been bathed, so have a towel handy to wrap him in as soon as you have finished.

3 Apply dog shampoo by putting a small amount on your hand or using a sponge and lathering well. Massage the shampoo gently into the dog's skin. Rinse all the suds away and, if necessary, apply conditioner before rinsing again.

4 Lift the dog out and wrap him quickly in a towel. Ask your child to rub the dog down with the towel. If your dog will accept a hairdryer, use this on the lowest setting and move it in swift, wide movements over the dog's body to avoid scorching.

Having fun at
puppy playtime

Puppies learn a great deal from play, and it is a crucial part of their development. When they play with other dogs and puppies they learn how to relate to their own kind, read body language, use their teeth softly and cope with different sizes and breeds of dog. When they play with children and other family members, they should learn how to be confident but not over-boisterous.

Stay safe

Take into account your dog's breed when he is playing with your children. Too much rough-housing or tug-of-war style games can over-excite dogs, and they may become dangerous, particularly if they are larger breeds. Using toys, such as a ball or Frisbee, can help to exercise the dog and develop his coordination, and the toys can be used to start training him. Chasing games can over-stimulate dogs such as Border Collies, so channel their energies into something more constructive, such as negotiating obstacles and catching a ball and bring it back again.

A puppy's teeth can be needle sharp and will hurt if they are allowed to play-bite. A puppy often bites to relieve gum discomfort when new teeth are coming through, so providing him with teething toys to chew will help to discourage him from biting a nearby arm or leg. Thankfully, most puppies grow out of play-biting by the time they are about 20 weeks.

Come back!

Encourage your children to hide treats around the house or garden for the dog to find. Let him see them hiding them at first, but then make it more difficult by putting him in another room.

ABOVE: Terriers love soft toys — perfect for hunting down and 'killing'!

OPPOSITE ABOVE: Your child's relationship with the puppy can be strengthened if a favourite toy is reserved for her alone to offer to him.

OPPOSITE BELOW: Encourage your puppy to become a sleuth. Your child can hide a tasty treat in the corner of the house or garden and watch him track it down.

Tip to parents
You don't have to spend a fortune on toys for your puppy. A strong plastic lid can make a good substitute Frisbee, or visit your local charity store to find some cuddly soft toys.

Question time?

Q *When can I play with my dog?*
It's important to give your dog at least half an hour to digest his food before you allow your children to play with him. Two or three short play sessions scheduled throughout the day are better for dogs than one long, exhausting game, particularly for very young or old dogs, who may be prone to injuries or aches and pains.

A Wait for half an hour after his meal so that he can let his food go down properly. Dogs like lots of short games rather than one big long one, which might be tiring if he's only a baby or very old.

Ask the children to hide while you hold the dog, and then let him go with the command 'find'. When the dog finds his young owner he can be rewarded with a treat. These are good training games and can help the puppy get to know his name and assist with the recall command. Associating returning to someone when called and then receiving a treat or lavish praise and attention will reinforce the idea that humans are fun, and you will not experience problems trying to get him to come back to you when you call him (see pages 78–79).

It is important to remind children that not every game will be appropriate. Hide-and-seek, treasure hunts and obstacle races are all perfect, but activities like climbing trees and skateboarding are beyond the ability of most dogs! (See pages 90–91 for more ideas for games to play.)

Getting ready to
walk this
way

Walking is a great way for the family to get fit together and will help strengthen the relationship between you and your dog. It's also an ideal opportunity to practise some socialization and training techniques. Encourage your children to accompany you on walks as much as possible, even in bad weather, so that they develop a sense of responsibility and commitment.

Tip to parents
Invest in some high-visibility rainwear or cold-weather clothing so that your children are easily seen but remain dry and snug. High-visibility dog coats, leads and collars will help make winter walking safer for your dog.

Get the kids out there
Taking a regular part in dog walking will help strengthen your children's relationship with the puppy, and at the same time contribute to keeping them healthy. They will enjoy taking turns at holding the dog's lead, and you can give them treats and toys to reward the dog for coming when called. Other responsibilities can be allocated, such as carrying the dog's water bottle or cleaning up after the puppy (see opposite).

Question time

Q *I don't want to walk. I want to go and play with my friends.*

Dogs need to walk regularly every day to exercise and keep their joints fit and healthy. If children want the fun of owning a dog, they must understand the importance of this. You can take toys and treats with you on the walk and play games when you are out so that the dog and child have fun together. Try inviting your child's friends along on the walk and making a list of things to spot along the way, such as a particular type of tree, a flower or a local landmark. Make it a game for the children to find these items and tick them off on a list. If you make the walks fun experiences, your child will soon discover the joy of the great outdoors and the thrill of finding out just what makes the puppy happy.

A The dog will be sad if you don't walk him. He will also not be very healthy because he needs lots of walk to keep fit. Imagine if you were stuck indoors all the time, forced to watch the rest of the family playing. Why don't we invite some of your friends to come along, too. Can you think of some games we could all enjoy together? How about a treasure hunt!

How far should we go?

How far you walk and how often will largely depend on the type of dog you have. Some of the working and pastoral breeds require more exercise than the smaller dogs, but even a Yorkshire Terrier is capable of enjoying quite a lengthy walk as long as he is fit and healthy.

The amount of exercise a dog needs will change over the years, and an older dog may gradually become reluctant to walk very far. However, gentle, frequent walks will help to keep him mobile and fit, so pop a warm coat on him and encourage him to join you outside despite his misgivings.

When you are walking puppies, try to plan the route so that at least half the walk is off hard ground. This will protect their pads and joints from over-exertion.

Clean up!

It is an antisocial act for dog owners not to clean up after their dogs, particularly when there are children in the area. Dog faeces can contain bacteria that can be transmitted to children, either through direct contact or indirect contact, such as touching their shoes, which have been contaminated through walking in waste matter.

Kennel Clubs encourage children over the age of eight to be involved in picking up dog poo, so don't get your children used to the idea that this is something only adults do. When you go out, arm yourself with plastic bags or paper towels to pick up after your dog. Dispose of waste in dog bins or household waste, but do not put dog faeces on garden compost heaps because parasites can contaminate the compost.

chapter 5

Growing pains

Puppies have much in common with children. They love to enjoy themselves and express their joy at the simple things in life, and they are also sometimes naughty. This chapter looks at how you can involve your child in training a puppy, and how you can deal with bad behaviour from both the dog and your children.

A dog's world

Dogs can be confused by what children want them to do, particularly if they shriek when they are excited and call the dog's name repeatedly. Teaching your children to read canine body language will enable them to understand how your dog communicates and help to make them safer around all dogs, because they will know how to read the signals that a dog is feeling fearful or defensive (see pages 64–65).

To help your children understand how a dog thinks, ask them to pretend to be a dog and imagine how the world will look from a dog's point-of-view. Remind them that a dog cannot use words to tell us how he is feeling, but must rely on other communication skills. He will use his eyes and highly developed senses of smell and hearing to help him work out whether something is friendly or likely to taste good and whether he recognizes someone. To communicate that he is happy or sad, a dog will use his tail, body language, facial expression, hackles and voice.

Pack animals

Dogs generally adore the company of people, so to be isolated from family life for long periods is something that will make them miserable. Unfortunately, untrained dogs are such a nuisance that they are often kept apart from the family, which exacerbates their behaviour problems.

In the wild, dogs are pack animals, and they need to be able to cooperate with each other in order to survive. However, our canine companions don't always understand what we expect from them, so it is important to explain as clearly as possible. For example, if you give the command 'down' when you want him to jump off a chair or stop jumping up at someone, and then give the 'down' command when you want him to lie down, you will confuse him. How can he know whether you want him to jump down off the chair or lie down and get comfy? To avoid confusion, use clear, separate commands, such as 'down' when you want him to lie down and 'off' when you want him to get off a chair.

Can you tell
how a
dog feels?

A closer look at your dog's body language will reveal many clues about how he is feeling. As the whole family gets to know the dog, it will become obvious when he is feeling relaxed and when he is nervous or alarmed. Discuss the signs with your children so they do not try to play with him when he is not in the mood.

ABOVE: A dog lying on his side with legs extended is feeling tired, but relaxed and secure in his surroundings.

OPPOSITE: If your child looks at the puppy while stroking him or giving a treat, the dog will learn that eye contact with her is not a threat.

Tip to parents
Spending time as a family observing your dog when he is happy will help you to recognize those times when he is feeling less confident or threatened by a new and unpredictable situation.

Body language
If the dog is happy and relaxed his eyes will appear soft, not particularly wide and staring, and he will not show the whites of his eyes (unless, of course, they are always visible). His ears will be relaxed — that is, neither directly upright nor flat down. When he lies down, his legs will probably be stretched out to the side, showing that he is happy to lie in this vulnerable position rather than defensively, with his legs tucked underneath ready to leap up and run.

The tail of a happy, relaxed dog is usually up and wagging confidently from side to side as your child plays and interacts with him. It is the human equivalent of shaking your hand when he meets you. A dog that bows towards his owner, with his front end down and back end up in the air, as he wags his tail and perhaps barks, is usually asking for someone to please play a game with him.

If your dog is worried, perhaps because he has met a strange dog for the first time, his tail may be clamped down between his legs. However, if he is feeling aggressive he may fluff up his tail, holding it up and straight out, and he may also raise his hackles, lift his lips and growl intermittent warnings, and make staring eye contact.

He's smiling!

Children always think that smiling means that someone is pleased to see them. If they see a dog curling his lips, they may assume that he is happy to see them. However, this is not always the case. In the dog world, it can mean that the dog is feeling a little uncertain. Some breeds of

Do! Encourage your child to …

* Observe her dog and try to guess how he's feeling
* Understand how a dog communicates
* Recognize that confused dogs can give out mixed messages
* Get the dog to look at her when they are playing together or offering a treat
* Say the dog's name only once when she asks him to do something

Don't! encourage your child to …

* Assume she knows exactly how a dog is feeling
* Make prolonged eye contact with a strange dog
* Shout a dog's name repeatedly

dog, such as a Dobermann and many of the terriers, have a reputation for smiling. Their lips curl up and they show their teeth when they see you so that they do, indeed, look happy. In some cases, this kind of smiling is a sign of submission. However, it is not an aggressive act and there is nothing to worry about.

Working for treats and rewards

To help your dog learn to behave well among children and other dogs and to adapt to family life, it is important to develop a positive, reward-based training system. Children are familiar with the concept of rewards for work that has been well done, but they are not always certain how to reward their dog. Special toys and healthy treats are much better than things like sweets and cookies.

Food

Dogs are greedy creatures, and food treats are always welcome. Try to get into the habit of offering treats only for work well done, so that they retain their importance. If you or your child offer treats from a plate just because the dog is asking, you will be rewarding him for begging, and there will be less significance attached to the rewards given during training.

Small pieces of cooked sausage, chicken, liver, cheese and tasty dog treats are all suitable rewards in training. Avoid using high-calorie human food, because these will disrupt your dog's calorie intake and lead to weight gain. When you are training your dog and using a lot of treats, remember to factor this into his daily calorie intake to make sure he isn't consuming too many.

Toys

Experiment to see what types of toy motivate your dog most. He may prefer squeaky, noisy toys, a ball or hoop or tug-of-war toys, so experiment to find out which are his favourites. Keep one or two in a special place, out of reach from the dog, to use as rewards. Only allow access to these toys for short periods when he has behaved particularly well.

Playtime

Another reward that your dog will appreciate is time off from work to simply play and have fun. Separate training and socialization sessions by scheduling short bursts of play, such as throwing and retrieving a ball or Frisbee. This kind of interactive play, involving your children, will help to teach the dog respect and self-discipline as he learns not to engage in chasing or play-biting.

ABOVE: Dogs love a quick snack and will be all the more eager to obey commands if they know treats are around!

OPPOSITE ABOVE: For maximum effect, find out which toys motivate your dog most.

OPPOSITE BELOW: Sometimes a stroke and a cuddle is just what your dog wants.

Child's-eye view
'I think my dog would like a cookie if he behaved well.' Melissa, age 7

Tip to parents
Providing healthy treats (rather than cookies) means that edible rewards can be given more frequently without damaging your dog's health.

Question time

Q *How can I let my dog know when he's done something well?*
There are several different types of reward, and it is important to give them each time the dog does something well to encourage a particular behaviour and motivate him to repeat it. In the early days of helping your children to become potty-trained you would give plenty of verbal praise every time they asked to go or successfully passed a dry night. It is the same with dogs: reward even the smallest of breakthroughs, particularly for complicated tasks.

A You get stickers and stars at school, but dogs need different rewards, such as toys, treats and lots of praise in a happy voice. When we are training him to do something we need to give him lots of rewards every time he gets it right, then we can gradually give him less.

Good dog!

One of the most effective rewards is verbal praise, stroking and a generally positive reaction. All this fuss is a cheap, no-calorie technique, guaranteed to make your dog happy. Teach your children to adopt a happy, excited tone when they are praising the dog and a sterner, deeper tone to discourage him. Remind them that dogs have a limited understanding of words and that the tone of voice is always more important. A simple 'good dog' is much more effective than a lengthy description of what he has done right.

Teach children that rewarding a dog for good behaviour can help to ensure that he behaves well in the future. He doesn't have to be doing anything spectacular to be praised. It is also useful to praise him simply for being calm in certain situations, such as when another dog walks past. When a dog does not behave in the way a child wants him to, it is important not to resort to shouting or smacking as this will merely confuse the dog and make him less likely to respond. Show the child how to use distraction with toys or treats to refocus the dog's attention.

Dealing with
tantrums
and tears

Young children – and some older children, too – can be prone to temper tantrums, often caused by frustration at not getting what they want. Sometimes they rail at something they perceive to be unfair. A toddler is likely to be enraged if another child takes a favourite toy from them, for example, and they may react in a similar way if their dog does the same thing.

Keep your eyes open

Unfortunately, reason often goes out of the window during a tantrum, and the child may resort to violence if the dog takes a favourite toy, perhaps picking up another toy and whacking the dog over the head. It is important to protect your dog from these outbursts, because no matter how good-natured a dog is he will have his mental breaking point. Some dogs will react with fear, running away and hiding from the child, whereas others may react by snapping and biting, which is, of course, dangerous.

The importance of supervision cannot be overstated. Young children are at eye-contact level and their faces are vulnerable. If a fraught

Do!
- Supervise children and dogs constantly
- Teach patience
- Ask children to tidy up toys, particularly small ones that could be swallowed
- Deal promptly with tantrums by removing the child from the situation
- Explain the consequences of tantrums and how this could make the dog react

Don't!
- Set a bad example to your child by using physical punishment
- Allow the dog access to some children's toys and not others
- Give the dog old shoes, socks or items of clothing to chew – he will not be able to differentiate between these and new clothes

situation develops, remove the child as soon as possible, and then turn your attention to the dog, perhaps by trying to retrieve the toy he has grabbed by distracting him with one that he is allowed to have.

Coping with frustration

Owning a dog helps young children learn the concept of patience, and is a good way of encouraging them to develop strategies to cope with frustration. Even very small children must learn that it is never acceptable to hit out at a dog, pull his ears, poke him or in any way be violent. Adopt a zero-tolerance attitude to this, and take the child to a safe, dog-free room. However, it is important to explain why such behaviour is unacceptable and the possible dangerous consequences, and then try to think of better and safer ways for the child to deal with frustration – perhaps by coming to find an adult to deal with the situation properly.

ABOVE: Encourage your child to keep all her toys tidied away, so that the dog doesn't become confused about which toys belong to him.

OPPOSITE: Any dog can bite if sorely provoked. All interactions between young children and dogs should be supervised, to ensure that tempers do not fray.

Question time

Q *My dog is really stupid. He won't come when I call him!*
Children can get frustrated if a dog doesn't do something for them, particularly if he does it immediately for another family member.

A He's not being stupid. It's a bit like when I ask you to get ready for school in the mornings and you're busy doing something else, like daydreaming, playing on the computer, watching television or generally feeling too tired or bored. There are lots of reasons why a dog won't do as he is told, but the more we can make training fun for him the better he will do.

chapter 6

Training for kids

This chapter shows how children can be involved in all aspects of training, from the basics needed for good canine behaviour to advanced tricks, such as jumping through hoops. Start training your dog early. The sooner he learns how to respond to his name, to come when he is called and to sit or lie down on command, the more you can enjoy having him as a family member. Make everyone in the family uses the same basic commands, so that the dog isn't confused.

Standing tall

If you have chosen a large breed, young children will often be smaller than the dog when he reaches adulthood. Standing taller than another dog or pinning another dog down is one of the ways that dogs determine who is the more dominant. It is important to start training as a puppy so that this does not become a problem. If you have a large dog, sit the child on your knee and encourage him to pet the dog from this elevated position. Always discourage rough play that involves the dog chasing the child, nipping or jumping up.

Bear hugs

The muzzle and scruff of a dog's neck are very sensitive. When the dog was a puppy, this is where his mother would hold him to assert her authority, and when dogs fight attention is focused on the head. If a child grabs a dog around the head or envelops his neck in a bear hug it could be perceived as threatening, and the dog may react aggressively. Encourage your children to pet the dog gently on his back. This will subtly reinforce the child's dominant position in the family hierarchy.

Quietly does it

When children are excited their voices become high-pitched and their body movements are often erratic. If they are holding their arms up, a dog may think they are inviting him to jump up. Training a dog to lie down or sit on command is important to prevent this.

Children sometimes repeat a dog's name so often that the dog 'tunes out' completely and ignores them. Encourage your children to say the dog's name once and reward him with a treat or a toy as soon as he pays attention to them.

What's in a name?

The children will want to be involved in choosing a name for your dog. Bear in mind that the best names are short, with one or two syllables, and that it must be easy to say and shout. Remember, too, that at many veterinary surgeries your dog's name will be tagged on to your surname, so if you think it might be embarrassing to have the practice nurse shout out something like 'Cutie Pie Jones' or 'Sneezy Smith' in the middle of a busy waiting room, it might be time for a rethink.

Paws
for thought

Sit up and beg, shake paws and high five are great tricks that will delight your children and boost their street-cred. Dogs must learn to balance to do these tricks, so warn children not to be too enthusiastic or they will push the dog over and make him lose confidence. As with all training, involve your children if they are old enough but also supervise them, especially in the early stages.

Sit up and beg

1 Your child should begin by teaching the dog to sit up and beg. She should put the dog in a sit and stand or kneel in front of him, holding a treat out towards his nose.

2 The child should move her hand up and back slightly so that the dog tilts his head backwards and lifts his front paws off the ground. As soon as both paws come off the ground, she should click and reward.

3 She should repeat the procedure several times, each time asking the dog to lift his paws a little higher until he eventually finds his point of balance. She can begin to withhold the click and treat for a second or two to encourage him to remain up on his haunches. A verbal command, such as 'beg', 'both' or 'say please', can be built in to trigger the move.

Shake on it

Your child should put the dog into a sit and kneel in front of him, holding a treat in her hand so the dog can smell it. She should move her hand slightly so he shifts his weight from the paw she wants him to lift. Most dogs will lift a paw to try to get the treat and, if he does, she should click and treat. If he seems reluctant, she can pick up his paw, click and treat.

Ask her to keep practising, adding a verbal command just before she clicks and using separate words for each front paw, such as 'paw' for the right and 'pat' for the left. She can develop the trick by holding a treat in one hand and opening out her other hand next to the paw she wants the dog to lift, clicking and treating as soon as he does so. Eventually the dog will learn that he gets a reward for lifting his paw when he sees the child's open hand.

High five

This trick is basically the same as giving a paw, but instead of holding her palm out your child should turn her hand over in a high five. Click and treat as soon as the dog makes contact, building in the command 'high five'. With practice the dog should be able to do a nice pat-a-cake rhythm using both paws. As a variation, your child can put the dog into a beg and hold both her hands out in a high five, clicking as the dog touches both hands at the same time and then rewarding.

ABOVE: Your child will impress her friends no end if she can shake paws and do a high five with her dog!

Do! encourage your child to …

- Take her time and practise these moves so that the dog will eventually respond to visual cues
- Kneel down if necessary and get close enough to the dog to make it easy for him to make contact with her hands

Don't! encourage your child to …

- Try sit up and beg or a high five before the dog is six months old or his developing joints could be damaged
- Ask older dogs with joint problems to do upright tricks
- Expect young dogs or large breeds to be able to balance immediately; it may be necessary to hold a paw to steady the dog at first

chapter 7

Health and safety

This chapter looks at basic hygiene and safety rules, from getting rid of fleas to protecting your dog outside the home. Some diseases can be passed on to children by dogs, so it is important to make children aware that they must wash their hands after touching a dog, particularly before meals. Small children often think that turning the tap on and off constitutes hand washing, so supervise them to make sure they use soap and water thoroughly.

Worming

The most common parasitic worms in dogs are roundworms and tapeworms. A puppy who is infested with roundworms looks sickly and has a pot-belly. The roundworms are sometimes vomited and resemble pale, curled elastic bands. There are two types, *Toxocara canis* and *Toxascaris leonine*, but only the worms of *T. canis* can be passed to humans. Although it is rare, the eggs can survive in soil for up to four years, so keeping your garden cleared of dog faeces is important.

The eggs of tapeworms resemble grains of rice, and if your dog is infested they may be visible around the anus. The tapeworm attaches itself to the wall of the dog's intestine, and the eggs are excreted in faeces.

Don't forget that telling children they could catch worms from the dog will probably make them think of earthworms! Explain that these are special worms, called parasites, which live inside the dog. Although it is quite rare for children to become infested by the family pet, a child may come into contact with the parasite in playgrounds or parks where dog fouling has occurred and the faeces have not been removed.

Worm eggs can cause toxicariasis (sometimes called toxocara), which can cause allergic reactions and even blindness. Some worms cause hydatid disease, which affects the liver, lungs and brain, although this is more prevalent in sheep-farming areas. Toxicariasis is extremely dangerous to pregnant women because it can cause major damage to, or even the death of, the foetus.

Thankfully, worming products obtained from your vet are extremely effective at killing worms. These are given orally or as spot-on treatments, when a tiny amount is squirted on to the dog's neck. A puppy should have been wormed when he was two or three weeks old to kill any parasites that were passed to him in his mother's milk. Worm your child's dog regularly – usually three or four times a year. Worming treatments will protect him when he comes into contact with other dogs and prevent the transmission of parasites.

Problems with
puppy passengers

'Are we nearly there yet?' There's a heartfelt plea that any parent will recognize. And, as any parent knows, a little forward planning can make the difference between a nightmare trip and a peaceful journey. When you are out and about travelling with your dog, whether it is on a short trip or a longer journey, you will need to plan and prepare just as meticulously.

Getting used to cars

Travelling in a car should be a vital part of the dog's socialization programme and will help make sure that he doesn't become distressed by it. As with children, never leave a dog unattended in your car because it can quickly become so hot that the dog dies.

You don't have to travel anywhere to get your dog used to being in the car. Simply sitting in a stationary car, while your child feeds him the odd treat and pets him quietly, will help. Once your dog is calm, you can take him on short drives, getting him out to do something he enjoys, such as a walk or a game in the park, before driving home again. If the only time he goes in the car is to do something stressful, such as visiting the vet, he will view travelling as a negative experience.

Some dogs are so eager to get into the car that they try to leap in before everyone else. This can be a nuisance, particularly if the dog is wet and muddy. From the beginning, put the dog into a sit and wait until you give him permission to get in (see pages 80–81 for the sit command).

Car safety

Children are much less vulnerable to injury when they are travelling if they wear a seatbelt, and it is also possible to buy special harnesses for dogs. If you have to do an emergency stop it can be extremely dangerous to have a dog hurtling from the back seat into the front, so a harness or dog guard is an excellent investment. A small dog can be transported in puppy crate.

Going on holiday

Some boarding establishments view themselves as proper dog hotels, offering services such as

swimming pools, heated towel rails and haute cuisine! However, a regular boarding kennel is fine, as long as it is clean and the facilities are good. Personal recommendation from a friend or vet is a good starting point. Before booking in your dog, you should check that the place is hygienic and the dogs well cared for. Find out if the dogs are exercised every day or are simply given access to a run. You should avoid anywhere that does not insist on up-to-date vaccination certificates before accepting a dog.

ABOVE: The dog should be trained to always go into a sit before entering the car.

OPPOSITE: Sitting quietly in the stationary car with your child will help your dog get used to being inside a vehicle.

Once you are happy, you can arrange for your dog to get to know the place during a one-day, two-day or overnight visit, so that the longer stay does not come as such a shock. Pack his own bed, toys and a sweater or fleece that smells of home so he has a 'comfort blanket' at night. Reassure your child that his dog will be kept warm and dry and fed and exercised regularly. You can explain that the dog will enjoy being in new surroundings with other dogs, and that you are sure he will be looked after safely.

Child's-eye view

'My dog loves being in the car. He sticks his head out of the window and his ears flap back, it's really funny.' Paul, age 8

Tip to parents

If you allow your dog to travel in the car with his head out of the window his eyes and ears are vulnerable to dust and debris. If is safer to put your dog in a harness so that he is not at risk.

How to be a garden explorer

A dog enjoys exploring the outside world and your children will be keen to show him all their secret dens and hiding places. However, small puppies are agile and capable of getting through tiny gaps. If the garden hasn't been properly dog-proofed he could escape, putting him at risk of disease from contact with other dogs (if he is unvaccinated) or injury from traffic.

Making the garden safe

Before you allow the dog into the garden, ask your children to go round every square inch of it, looking for small places that a puppy can hide or little gaps in the fence that he may be able to wriggle through.

- Ask children to make a 'please close the gate' notice, which you can laminate and position at child's-eye level to help remind them and their friends.
- Ask children to tidy away small toys or objects a dog might chew.
- Mend any holes or loose panels in fences.
- Check hedges and block up any gaps.
- Attach chicken wire or mesh to the bottom of metal gates that a small puppy could squeeze through.
- Consider re-hanging the gates so that they open inwards, making it more difficult for a dog to push his way out.
- Put locks on sheds and garages to keep out a curious dog.
- Put all chemicals, such as weedkiller, paints and antifreeze, on a high shelf; dogs are attracted to a chemical used in slug pellets, so be particularly careful with this product.
- Keep garage floors clean so that a puppy doesn't tread in anything chemical and ingest it later when he licks himself.

Poisonous plants

Some plants, such as bluebells, crocuses, foxgloves and wisteria, can be poisonous to puppies. However, if your dog is entertained by your children and having fun playing games it is unlikely he will be bored enough to start eating plants.

Run for it

Some people find it convenient to have an outdoor run and kennel area where they can put the dog occasionally when they have to go out. As long as this is a secure area, with a kennel containing a comfy bed, toys to play with and fresh water to drink, this can be a good solution. Dogs should not be left unattended for longer than four hours, however, or they can become bored and develop negative habits, such as prolonged barking or chewing.

First steps outside

Your children may be desperate to have the dog accompany them to school, but first he will have to complete his vaccinations. This usually happens at about 12 weeks. However, you should encourage the puppy to go into the garden to toilet as soon as you get him, so that he realizes this is the place to go. A small dog could always be carried to school occasionally, to experience the sights and smells along the way and to get used to being the centre of attention.

Tip to parents

Always make sure that your dog has access to fresh water when he is in the garden and that there is a sheltered area in which he can escape from strong sun or cold weather.

ABOVE: Boisterous games in the garden are a great way of using up surplus canine energy, and ensuring your child gets lots of exercise, too!

LEFT: Your child should help ensure that there is fresh water available for your dog when he is in the garden, whatever the time of year.

OPPOSITE: Keep dogs away from garden equipment and other potential dangers. Anything that might harm the puppy should be tidied away in a shed or other secure storage area.

Puppy safety
all year round

As your child's puppy grows, you will find that each season brings its own special joys. However, it's also useful to consider in advance the pitfalls that you might need to watch out for at different times of year. With determination and good planning, you will be able to avoid costly vet's bills and make sure that the dog enjoys year-round fun with the whole family.

Summer hazards

Make sure that your children are aware of the dangers that hot weather can pose for their dog. They might be enjoying themselves so much that they forget that the dog might not be having as much fun. Heat can be the worst problem. Dogs cannot perspire and quickly become overheated. Symptoms such as excessive panting, drooling and restlessness might require urgent veterinary attention. You should also ask your children to be vigilant that their dog doesn't get accidentally locked into a hot spot, such as a greenhouse. If he goes into the garden, there should be shaded areas to which he can retreat. Take him indoors to a cool room during the hottest part of the day. Extra grooming or a haircut can make your dog more comfortable in summer.

At any time of year, you should take plenty of fresh drinking water with you on long walks or if you are transporting your dog to the beach. Children can be responsible for carrying the travelling water bottle and offering water to the dog. They should stop the dog from drinking from stagnant ponds or puddles, which may contain toxic blue-green algae.

If your dog swims in the sea make sure you always wash him off afterwards, because dried sand and saltwater can irritate his skin. Make a note of tide times, and take care that he doesn't become exhausted. Boisterous games should be kept shorter than usual, because very young and older dogs don't always have the sense to stop when they are tired. The whole family will also need to supervise dogs carefully during picnics and barbecues, to make sure they don't eat something indigestible, such as a corn-on-the-cob husk or kebab stick.

Child's-eye view
'I want to build snowmen with my dog. We could make a snow dog too.' Annie, age 5

Tip to parents
Children and dogs playing in the snow are a joy to see, but limit the time they spend doing this. Snow sticks to a dog's coat and can ball up in his feet, so dry him off thoroughly when he comes indoors. Exposure to subzero temperatures can cause frostbite of the nose, ears and feet. If your dog's paws look red, grey or are peeling, wrap him in warm towels and seek veterinary advice.

Question time

Q *What should we do to help if an insect stings our dog?*
Bee and wasp stings usually occur on the dog's nose, mouth or paws. Some animals may have an allergic reaction, and if your dog suffers excessive swelling or difficulty breathing seek urgent attention. Bee stings are acid. If the sting is visible remove it with tweezers and bathe the area with a solution of bicarbonate of soda. Wasp stings are alkaline, and the sting is not left in the skin. Bathing with a weak solution of vinegar will soothe the affected area. If you suspect a snake has bitten your dog, contact your vet immediately.

A If you think an insect has stung the dog, try to find an adult to help. If you have seen what kind of insect it is, it will make the treatment easier. If we can see the sting we'll need to take it out carefully with tweezers and bathe the area to soothe it. Wasps don't leave their stings behind, but we can bathe the area to make it feel better. If the dog doesn't recover quickly or cannot breathe easily he may be having an allergic reaction, so we should take him to the vet.

ABOVE: A jacket will keep your dog warm on even the coldest days.

OPPOSITE: Dog water bottles have a specially designed trough that enables your puppy to drink when he is out and about. Access to fresh water is vital, whatever the season.

Winter blues

Your children will be wrapped up with scarves and gloves when they take their dog for a walk, but don't let them think that the dog's fur coat will be sufficient to keep him warm in the coldest weather. Wind chill can cause temperatures to drop sharply. Dogs with thin coats and older dogs with reduced body mass will need a coat in winter to keep them warm. Make sure that outdoor kennels are raised off the ground and are warm and free from draughts, but bring dogs inside as much as possible. Older dogs will appreciate an extra fleecy blanket on their beds.

After a walk, ask your children to wash the dog's paws in tepid water to remove ice, salt or grit. (If you keep the hair between your dog's toes trimmed, you will find it easier to spot anything hidden there.) You can also ask your children to check every day that the dog's water bowls do not ice over.

If your dog falls into an icy lake or river, get him out as fast as possible. He may be suffering from hypothermia, so wrap him in a warm blanket and seek veterinary advice.

Protect dogs and children from dangerous winter items. Put fireguards in place around fires and portable heaters, and make sure that heaters are out of reach. Store antifreeze and windshield wiper fluids safely; many are toxic but taste sweet, and your dog may be attracted to them.

chapter 8

What if?

Each phase of your dog's life will bring its pleasures and problems. This chapter examines some of the challenges and explores how children can help you deal with them. Even trained dogs can develop behavioural problems, such as excessive barking or fussy eating, or they might suffer from psychological difficulties, such as anxiety. The child-dog relationship can also become problematic at different times in the child's or dog's life. Given patience, these problems can be resolved.

Old age

As your dog enters his senior years he will need more care and attention. Thankfully, nutrition and veterinary medicine has advanced so much that dogs are living longer and now have an average age of about twelve years. Smaller dogs tend to live longer than the larger breeds, often carrying on happily into their late teens.

Nevertheless, as dogs grow older, they gradually slow down, particularly if they develop joint problems, such as arthritis. If your dog seems to be grumpier than usual when your children play with him, he may be reacting to pain. Your vet may be able to recommend special treatments and also give you some pain management tips that will help your dog enjoy life to the full for longer.

Dinner time

Pet-food manufacturers have developed a range of dog foods designed to fulfil the changing nutritional needs of older dogs. Older dogs tend to move around less and can therefore be prone to obesity, which increases the pressure on their joints. Make children aware that too many treats or human food snacks are not good for the dog.

Some veterinary surgeries run geriatric clinics for dogs, where blood pressure, weight and other vital signs are measured and you can get expert nutritional advice.

Exercise

An older dog can sometimes seem reluctant to go out, particularly in bad weather, but encouraging your children to take him out for regular, gentle exercise for short periods will help lubricate his joints and improve his mobility. Drying him off gently with a warm towel if he comes back wet will be appreciated, as will an extra blanket and a coat.

Explain to the children that their dog will not be able to play for as long or run as quickly as he grows older. Point out that it can be fun to think up games that have a slower pace, such as laying treasure trails of treats around the house, so that he can move from room to room looking for them rather than spending too long lying on his bed.

Putting your dog's bed somewhere in the middle of the home, such as the kitchen, will help him feel a part of family life even though he can't follow everyone around as he used to do. Ramps to get up and down to his favourite spot will also help make life easier for him.

When you need a little help

If your dog has previously been well behaved but suddenly develops behavioural problems, such as barking, biting, chewing or exhibiting signs of anxiety, it is important to find out the underlying cause of the new behaviour. Once this has been identified, the whole family should work together to help him overcome the problems.

Ask the vet

Many physical problems can cause changes in behaviour, so before you do anything else take the dog to your vet for a check-up to make sure that he has a clean bill of health. If the behavioural problems are very severe and badly affecting family life, your vet may recommend that he is referred to a professional animal behaviour counsellor for specific advice.

My dog's a bully!

If your dog starts guarding his food whenever anyone walks past him or growls when you want to take a toy from him, it's time to take action. Don't wait until the behaviour becomes deeply engrained or it will be much more difficult to change. Allowing your dog to rule the roost is a recipe for disaster. Make sure that your dog understands that he is not the leader of the family pack and that he knows his place in the family's pecking order (see pages 68–69).

Help! He won't get off my leg!

Mounting behaviour can be another sign of the dog trying to assert his dominance. You can deal with this embarrassing problem by following a behaviour modification programme that reinforces the dog's subordinate position in the family pack. Neutering may also be an answer (see page 69).

LEFT: Food guarding should be dealt with as early as possible, before behaviour such as snapping develops.

OPPOSITE: To kick the barking habit, praise your puppy when he is quiet and ignore him whenever he becomes very vocal.

Question time

Q *Why does the dog keep running off with my toys? He's got loads of his own.*
If your children run after the dog and chase him whenever he grabs one of their toys he will probably think it's a great game. Equally, if they snatch it off him and wave it in the air they will simply signal that they are keen for the game to continue. Try to explain that keeping calm and walking past the dog, dropping a food treat near him as a distraction or offering him one of his own favourite toys, will be a more effective way of getting him to leave their toys alone. Once he realizes that the only time he gets a game is when he plays with his own toys, he should start to leave your children's toys alone.

A He may think it's a game, especially if you run after him and try to grab it off him. Keep calm and fetch a food treat or one of the dog's special toys so that you can try to distract him. He needs to realize that he only gets to play with you if he is playing with his own toys.

Stop barking!

Dogs that bark incessantly can be real nuisances, for yourselves and for your neighbours. Behaviourists believe that attention-seeking behaviour, such as constant barking, tail chasing, paw chewing or licking, is best ignored as much as possible. As with children, rewarding attention-seeking behaviour with attention, even if it is very negative attention, will only help reinforce the behaviour you don't want.

The trick with barking is to reward the dog with praise and attention when he is quiet and calm and to walk away from him or put him in another room when he is not. If a particular situation triggers the barking, such as the doorbell ringing, you can enlist the help of your children to embark on a training programme. Ask the children to ring the doorbell and immediately tell the dog to go on his bed and give him a treat, such as food or a favourite toy. Practise this a lot so that the dog begins to associate the doorbell ringing with going to his bed and getting a treat.

Flushing out
toilet
trouble

Dogs are usually easy to house-train, particularly if your child has had him from a puppy and has consistently taken him outside when he wakes up or has finished eating. However, problems can still arise. Puppy training pads are a temporary indoor solution, but don't rely on them for too long or you will have difficulty in persuading your puppy to go outside.

Training regimes

Remind your child that puppies have smaller bladders than larger dogs and find it more difficult to retain urine, so they will need to go outside more often. Don't withhold water from the dog at night to try to toilet-train him: water is vital for hydration and optimum health.

Your child should stay calm and patient when house-training a dog. Shouting or physically punishing him will make him anxious and exacerbate the problem so the process takes even longer. Behaviourists have observed that fear and excitement are two of the main causes of incontinence, although an older dog may simply have trouble getting to the door in time. If this is the case, you may have to wake him up and take him outside before he leaves it too long. Rescue dogs who have been in a shelter for a long time may need to be completely retrained, although some get the hang of things very quickly.

In recent years, some manufacturers have developed pheromone-enriched markers to train dogs to urinate in a specific place outdoors. This pheromone is a synthetic version of a natural substance produced by dogs. The post is simply pushed into a grassy area of the garden to encourage dogs to go there.

Clean up

Older children can help you to clean any areas where your dog has an accident, mopping thoroughly with a suitable stain- and odour-removing product. Explain that this will get rid of the smell and help deter him from going there again. It might be a good idea to remove the puppy calmly from the room before cleaning up, as your body language might communicate

Tip to parents
Make sure that someone accompanies the puppy every time he goes outside so that you can be certain he does toilet and can be praised immediately.

Question time

Q *Why is our puppy dry in the day but not at night?*
It may be some weeks before your puppy can go all night without emptying his bladder. Newspaper or a toilet training pad near the door help minimize mess. If you put a puppy in an indoor crate at night, he will be reluctant to soil his own sleeping area, although this will not help him learn to go to the door.

A It's just because he's little and can't go all through the night yet. You were the same when you were very small. We need to take him out as much as possible and put some newspapers on the floor by the door or in his crate so that he learns that this is the correct place to go.

annoyance and frighten the puppy, making him more likely to be nervous and make toileting mistakes in the future.

Watch it!

As with other behaviour problems, take your dog to the vet for a check-up if toilet-training problems develop suddenly. Once he has the medical all-clear, you can investigate possible causes and try to rectify the situation. A change in

the dog's routine may have caused a setback in training. Tell your children that feeding at the same time each day and taking him outside within 20 minutes of eating is very important, because this is usually when a puppy needs to open his bowels. When a puppy first arrives, he should be taken outside every couple of hours.

Everyone should learn the signs that your dog needs to toilet. He may start sniffing, circling or even go to the door and scratch at it, and this is when your child can take him outside and give him a verbal command, such as 'toilet'. She should try to get the puppy to walk outside rather than carrying him out, because this will help him learn to go to the door and ask to go out. She should give her dog lots of praise every time he goes in the right place.

ABOVE: Encourage your child to get in the habit of taking the dog outside when he wakes up and after every meal.

LEFT: Any traces of an accident indoors should be thoroughly mopped up, so the smell doesn't encourage the puppy to repeat the performance.

OPPOSITE: Scratching at the door is a sign that your puppy wants to go outside to toilet.

Fussy eaters
and greedy guts

As parents we love to see our children enjoying the right sort of healthy food and leaving empty plates. When this happens the effort involved in preparing nutritious meals seems worthwhile. However, children are certainly not always interested in eating the food that we think is good for them, and dogs can sometimes be just as fickle.

Fuss pots

Some owners have reported that their dogs refuse to eat the food in their bowl unless they are spoon-fed. Unfortunately, as with young children, rewarding fussy eaters with extra attention or a range of several choices and flavours, simply makes the situation worse.

If your dog is a fussy eater, first take him to the vet for a physical check-up to rule out a medical cause for his behaviour. Once he has the all-clear it is probably time for you to adopt a tough-love approach to his diet.

Choose a complete dog food (which provides all the nutrition that your dog needs) and put his daily portion down in a clean dish at meal times. Explain to your children why they shouldn't try to hand-feed him or pay extra attention to him if he turns up his nose at what they are offering. After twenty minutes, if the food hasn't been eaten, simply remove and dispose of it. Wet food deteriorates very quickly, particularly in hot weather, and bacteria may affect its palatability, so don't be tempted to keep it until the next day.

Most dog behaviourists predict that repeating this exercise over a few days will soon produce an improvement in your dog's eating habits. Make sure that your children are not sneaking the dog treats or things from their own plates because they feel sorry for him or because they want to off-load things they don't fancy eating themselves.

LEFT: Energetic games in the park are a fun way of keeping dogs and children healthy.

OPPOSITE: A greedy dog may even knock over the kitchen rubbish bin to see what tasty treats are lurking inside. Dispose of left-over food securely so that he isn't tempted to forage.

Too fat

If you take your dog for an annual check-up, your vet will weigh him and tell you if he is putting on too much weight. Obesity is just as dangerous for dogs as it is for children and adults, so step up his exercise programme, reduce his calorie intake and encourage your children to play with him more so that he regains his fitness. One of the best things about owning a dog is that it can help everyone in the family keep fit.

On the scrounge

Dogs are natural scavengers and they may knock over rubbish bins, or even work the foot pedal, in order to get at the contents, even if they are fed sufficient food by their owners. They may ingest things that are potentially dangerous to them, such as bones or plastic packaging. If this is a problem, get a strong bin with a lid that is difficult to open or reposition the bin into a locked cupboard or utility room.

Child's-eye view

'I sometimes daydream when I'm eating, especially if I'm watching the television, and then our dog sneaks up and eat things off my plate. It makes me mad but I still love him.'
Andrew, age 9

Tip to parents

Some dogs are tempted by the smell of food, and if your dog is a bit of a thief it may be easiest to shut him out of the room when the children are eating. Discourage your children from wandering around while they eat because the sight of a chocolate bar or jam tart being paraded at eye level might prove irresistible!

Encouraging him to
be brave

There are many examples of how courageous dogs can be. Even small dogs can be brave when it comes to protecting their owners and homes from intruders. However, it's important that your children recognize that all dogs are different and that their tolerance levels to things such as noise will vary — some appear oblivious, whereas others are terrified.

Fright night

Sometimes fear can affect dogs so much that they will run off in a panic and are unable to find their way home again, which can be distressing for everyone. Fireworks are used in celebrations at various times throughout the year, and thunder and lightning storms can make some dogs tremble with nerves.

You may be able to pinpoint your dog's initial bad experience, perhaps when he was a puppy, or it may be something that you will never understand. Whatever the reason for his fear, a desensitization programme is far more effective than rewarding negative reactions with extra cuddles and praise.

Question time

Q *How do we find our dog?*
If your dog goes missing, get your children to make posters with an up-to-date photograph of the dog. Distribute them in your neighbourhood. Put fliers through your neighbours' doors asking them to check outbuildings. An advertisement in your local paper or on the radio may also yield results. Report him missing to the company that holds your dog's microchip database and inform your vet, local animal shelters, police and the dog warden. Search areas repeatedly at different times of the day, and if necessary offer a reward.

A There's a lot we can do. You can help by making posters and pinning them to trees and gateposts. We need to let as many people as possible know that he's missing, so tell all your friends and ask them to help look for him too. We'll stand a much better chance of getting him home safely if we search different areas at different times. We'll also put an advert in the paper, and we mustn't forget to tell his microchip company and the vet.

If your dog always runs and hides behind the sofa every time he hears a loud noise it can be tempting to pull him out and comfort him, but this simply reinforces his behaviour. Ask everyone to ignore him and behave as normally as possible, so that the dog does not pick up messages that he is right to be worried. Try to send out relaxed signals, such as yawning, lying down or slow blinking, and don't stare at the dog even if he is looking to you for reassurance. He will pick up on your body language, so make sure the message is, 'It's all ok, there's nothing to worry about.'

If your dog shows extreme fear your vet may suggest testing his hearing to make sure he has no hypersensitivity to noise. A low dose of tranquillizers may provide a short-term solution, but desensitization is the best long-term plan.

Desensitize
You can buy a plug-in dog-appeasing pheromone (DAP) dispenser, which some dogs find calming,

although it is useful only if you can predict when a storm or firework display is due to start. The pheromones are synthetic versions of natural substances produced by lactating bitches three to five days after birth, to relax and reassure the pups, so by plugging in a DAP you will remind your puppy subconsciously of mum. Your vet may be able to supply or source these for you.

Listen up
Specialists in animal behaviour have developed CDs that have been designed to accustom pets gradually to the particular sound that frightens them, whether it is fireworks or thunder. Your child can simply play the CD at the lowest level when the dog is doing something pleasurable, such as eating, playing a game or being stroked. Gradually, over the next few days and weeks, ask your child to increase the volume until the dog tolerates the noise without fearful reactions, such as panting, trembling, licking his lips or hiding.

Mediating child-dog relations

The relationship between a child and her dog is not always smooth. Problems range from pestering the animal to being jealous of the attention it receives, or ignoring it completely as the child grows older. If problems are left for too long they become difficult to resolve, so act quickly. Your vet may have useful advice or be able to recommend an experienced behaviourist or counsellor.

My teenage son ignores the dog

When children grow into young adults they may consider demonstrations of affection towards the family pet as 'uncool', childish behaviour. However, if anything were to happen to the dog they would no doubt be just as upset as anyone else. If your child has responsibilities for the dog's care, such as walking or feeding, these should continue or it will affect the dog's wellbeing. Otherwise, provided your dog gets attention from other family members, he should not be too affected by this passing phase in your teenager's life.

The youth section of your national Kennel Club will have many teenage members who are involved in fun and exciting activities. Find out if there is anything planned for your area that might interest your teenager.

My daughter pesters the dog

Some dogs are tolerant of childish attention, but others are less so. Older dogs can develop joint problems and may express pain in a grumpy, growling way. Explain that your dog doesn't appreciate being handled all the time, especially if she is carrying him everywhere, as it makes him feel insecure. Agree on when play times will be and how long they will last and encourage her to involve the dog in interactive games, such as fetching a ball, so that they engage with each other positively. Afterwards, try to find fun activities to distract your daughter from the dog.

Our kids have lost interest now the puppy is fully grown

Think of some activities they can do together, such as throwing a party for their friends and dogs (see pages 94–95). Vary walk routes so they

aren't boring and ask your children where they'd like to go. Explain that the dog is a family member, not a toy that can be abandoned, and encourage them to become responsible owners.

My child is jealous of our puppy

Pets and children need time to get used to each other, so supervise them carefully. Encourage your child to play with the dog. Give your child lots of attention, positively reinforcing her behaviour with praise, so that it is an enjoyable experience. Ignore unwanted behaviour, such as sulking, as much as possible, using distraction techniques to divert her attention in a positive way.

My son's friend is scared of dogs

You probably need to contact the boy's parents and find out their attitude towards dogs. If they are communicating their own fears it will be harder for your child's friend to overcome his anxiety. Some children are afraid that the dog will knock them over or bite them, and it may be that in time this boy will feel reassured that your dog is well behaved and harmless.

My nephew is allergic to dogs

Despite your best efforts, your nephew may experience some allergic reaction, so make sure

that he has enough medication for any visits, particularly sleepovers. If he is coming for a short visit try to keep the dog in an outdoor kennel, and vacuum the house thoroughly at least two hours beforehand. Vacuuming just before a visit is worse than doing nothing at all because it takes two hours for the dust to settle, and the dust could trigger an attack as much as the dog hairs. Don't forget to vacuum all the curtains and loose covers, which are dust traps and often forgotten. Damp-dusting with a weak solution of water and vinegar will help rid your house of dust.

What if a dog chases your child?

Teach your child to 'act like a tree' – that is, stand very still and quietly. Running away will simply encourage the dog to chase after her. If she is sitting down or is knocked down by a dog, the child should 'act like a rock', curling up on one side with her fists over her ears. If she is afraid the dog is going to bite, encourage her to throw something as bait, such as a backpack or jacket.

If your child is on a bicycle, the spinning of a bike's wheels and pedals may excite the dog. Encourage your child to stop her bike and dismount, saying 'no' loudly. If she has a water bottle, a spray of this towards the dog may help distract him.

ABOVE: If you have more than one child, you may find that one sibling becomes jealous of a new puppy and its bond with the other sibling. Make sure you give everyone in the family lots of attention.

OPPOSITE: When children become teenagers, they may lose interest in the dog. Give the dog lots of extra love and allow the teenager space while the phase passes.

Saying goodbye
and hello

Ideally, your dog will enjoy a long and happy life with your family, and it is everyone's dream that a beloved older dog will simply die in his sleep, so that nobody has to make a decision about euthanasia. However, accidents and illness or deterioration in the dog's quality of life sometimes mean that euthanasia is the most humane step for you to take.

ABOVE: Drawing pictures of their pet and writing about him can help children come to terms with their grief at his death.

OPPOSITE: As an animal ages or becomes ill, your child may be distressed that he can no longer play with her in the old way. Explain that he is at a stage in his life when he needs special care from his family.

Grief

The loss of a family pet is often a child's first experience of death and grieving, and how much you explain about what has happened will depend on the child's age and level of emotional maturity. A child may be much more stalwart and accepting than many adults and often copes better as a result. If your dog is very old, you can try to prepare children for the inevitable, so that it does not come as a complete shock. It's best to avoid the phrase 'the dog was put to sleep', as this can make young children anxious about going to sleep themselves.

Psychologists recognize that there are several distinct phases to the grieving process for both adults and children:

- **Anticipated loss** This occurs particularly with a very old dog or one who has had a prolonged illness.
- **Shock and denial** These reactions are common immediately after death, particularly if a healthy dog has been involved in an accident.
- **Emotional suffering** The familiar middle phase, when crying and talking about the dog can seem very painful.
- **Recovery** This stage occurs when, finally, your child can accept the situation and it is possible to move on.

If your child seems stuck in any stage of the grieving process your vet may be able to offer a bereavement counselling service. Alternatively, your doctor may recommend a specialist counsellor. Encouraging children to write and talk about the dog, draw pictures or make a photo album will all be helpful. Tell your child's teacher if you have lost a family pet.

When is it time?

Talk to the vet about your dog's quality of life and if there is anything more he can to do to help. Generally, if a dog is in constant pain, is unable to move, cannot eat or drink properly or is totally incapacitated it may be kindest to let the vet intervene. Euthanasia is a painless procedure, involving an injection to put the dog to sleep and then a second one to stop his heart. It takes seconds, and vets are very experienced at dealing with it. Most encourage owners to be present if they wish. Beforehand, consider whether you want to take the dog home to bury him in the garden or if you want a cremation.

Question time

Q *Can I have another dog?*
When everyone in the family accepts the loss of the dog and can talk about him without sadness you might be able to welcome another one into your life. However, no dog will ever replace one that you have owned for years, and you might like to get another breed or type of dog to avoid comparisons. If your circumstances have changed, consider if you can offer another dog a loving home for life. See the first chapter of this book for advice on what your dog will need.

A We need to be sure that everyone in the family is not still so sad that they don't give a new dog all the love he deserves. And we need to think about what kind of dog we'd like, because we'll never get another one like Toby, and it wouldn't be fair to expect a new dog to be just like him. Perhaps choosing another breed altogether will make it easier. Let's think about the kind of dog can we give a home to.

Index

Page numbers in *italics* refer
to illustrations.

A
abdomen, health checks *4`5*
accidents, car 103
activity toys 91
adenoviral hepatitis 101
adult dogs, choosing 19
advantages of dog ownership 12–13
aggression, signs of 30, 65
agility training 92–3, *92–3*
algae, blue-green 108
allergies 13, 109, 121
anal glands 49, 53
animal welfare centres 16–17, 21
animals, introducing puppy to 49
antifreeze, safety 109
antisocial behaviour 69, 112
arthritis 111
attention-seeking behaviour 113

B
babies, jealousy of 13
bad habits 41
bags, doggy 28, *28*
balls 58
barbecues 108
barking 113, *113*
bathing 33, 54–5, *54–5*
beaches 108
Beagle 90
bear hugs 73
bedding 33, 109
beds 27, 33, *41*, 111
bedtime routines 47
bee stings 109
begging 50
  discouraging 66, 85
  sit up and beg 88, 88
behaviour problems 22, 68–9, 112–13
  see also training
benefits of dog ownership 12
Bichon Frise 29
bicycles, chasing 103, 121
birthday presents, puppies as 13
bitches, smell 53
bites
  discouraging 121

play biting 58
  safety 25
boarding kennels 101, 104–5
body language 63
  aggression 30, 65
  relaxed dogs 64–5
  smiling 65
  strange dogs *24*
  tails 65
  warning signals 30
bone injuries 39
Border Collie *11*, 19, *29*, 58, 85, 92, 103
Border Terrier 20
Bordetella bronchiseptica 101
boredom 107
bottoms, smelling other dogs' 49
bowls 33
boxes, puppy beds 33, *41*
breeders
  buying puppies 20, 21
  collecting puppy from 34
  socializing puppies 31
breeds, choosing *13*, 16, 19
bristle and pin brushes 52
brushes 33, 52
bubble trails 90–1, *90*
bullying 112
burial 123
buried treasure game 91
buying puppies 20–1

C
camps, training 77
canine parvovirus 101
canine rescue centres 16–17, 21
carpets, fleas in 101
carrots, as snacks 50
carrying dogs 28, 38–9, *38–9*
cars
  accidents 103
  chasing 103
  introducing puppy to 49
  overheating in 28, 104
  traffic safety 102–3, *102–3*
  travel in 104–5, *104–5*
cat flaps 35
cats, introducing puppy to 37
CDs, desensitizing dogs 119
chasing children 121
chasing games 58
chewing 23
chews, rawhide 50
Chihuahua 19, 29
child-dog relationships 120–1
chocolate 27, *27*

classes
  obedience 74
  puppy socialization 27
claws
  clipping 52
  health checks *45*
clicker training 33, 76–7, *76–7*
  coming back 78–9, *78–9*
  down command *85*
  roll over and die 86–7, *86–7*
  sit command 80, *80–1*
  stay command *82*
  tricks 89
clippers, nail 52
clothing, high-visibility 60
coat
  trimming 52
  in winter 109
  see also grooming
cold weather 109
collars 33, 74
  high-visibility 60, 103
combs 52
  defleaing dogs 33, *100*
commands
  confusing 63, 84
  down 84–5, *84–5*
  feeding puppy 50, *51*
  roll over 86, *86–7*
  sit 80, *80–1*
  stand 85
  stay 82–3, *82–3*
  wait 80
competitions
  agility training 92–3
  flyball 93
  heelwork to music (HTM) 96
complete dog foods 116
conditioners, coat 54
costs of keeping a dog 11
cotton wool 52
counselling
  behavioural problems 112
  grief 123
crates 27, 104
cremation 123
crossbreeds, buying 20–1

D
Dachshund *21*
dancing 96–7, *96–7*
dead, roll over and die trick 86–7
death 122–3
deciding to get a dog 9–17
desensitization, nervous dogs 118–19

diarrhoea 45
digging, buried treasure game 91
disadvantages of dog ownership 12–13
discipline 23
diseases
    vaccinations 26, 44, 100–1, *100–1*, 107
    from worms 99
distemper 101
distraction, in training 67
Dobermann 65
dog-appeasing pheromones (DAP) 119
dog-proof zone 34–5
doggy bags 28, *28*
dominant dogs
    behavioural problems 112
    establishing family hierarchy 22–3,
        68–9, 73
down command 84–5, *84–5*
dry foods 27, 50
drying dogs 33, 54, *55*

E
ears
    health checks *44*, 56
    relaxed dogs 64
eating habits 116
emotions
    grief 122–3
    puppy's 36
equipment, grooming 33, 52
euthanasia 123
excited children 73
exercise 28
    older dogs 111
    walking 60–1, *60*
eyes
    cleaning 52, *53*
    eye contact 25, 65, *65*
    health checks *44*, 56
    relaxed dogs 64

F
faeces
    picking up 61, *61*
    poop scoops 33
    toilet-training 115
    worm eggs in 99
family hierarchy 22–3, 69, 73, 112
fancy dress 94–5, 96
fashion accessories, dogs as 28
fat dogs 111, 117
fear
    of dogs 121
    nervous dogs 118–19, *118*
    signs of 30

feeding *see* food
feet *see* paws
female dogs, neutering 69, 112
fireguards 109
fireworks 118, 119
fleas 44, 45
    defleaing dogs *100–1*
    flea combs 33, 52
    treatments for 101
flyball 93
food
    bowls 33
    eating undisturbed 43
    fussy eaters 116
    guarding 112, *112*
    new puppies 50, *51*
    for older dogs 111
    playing after 59
    puppy's needs 26–7
    routines 47
    storing 33
    treats and rewards 66
frostbite 108
frustration, children 70–1
fussy eaters 116

G
games 58–9, 90–1, 95
gardens 106–7, *106–7*, 108
geriatric clinics 111
German Shepherd Dog 11, 97
giant dogs, choosing breeds 19
Golden Retriever 19, *20*
grass, eating 50
Great Dane 11, 85
greediness 50
greetings, licking 25
Greyhound 28–9, 85
grief 122–3
grooming *11*, 52–3, *52–3*
    bathing 33, 54–5, *54–5*
    equipment 33, 52
grooming mitts 52
growling 25, 30, 112
gums
    gum disease 56
    health checks *44*, 56

H
hair *see* coat
hairdryers 54
handling puppies 38–9, *38–9*
harnesses, car 104, 105
health
    health checks 27, *44–5*, 56–7

vaccinations 26, 44, 100–1, *100–1*, 107
    worming dogs 99
hearing, hypersensitivity to noise 119
heart, health checks *44*
heel, walking to 74, *75*
heelwork to music (HTM) 96–7, *96–7*
hepatitis, adenoviral 101
hide-and-seek games 58–9, 91
high five trick 89
hitting dogs 43, 71
holidays 104–5
hot weather 28, 108
house-training *10*, 37, 107, 114–15
housework 14
Husky *29*
hydatid disease 99
hygiene
    licking 25
    picking up faeces 33, 61, *61*
    see also safety
hypothermia 109

I
identity discs 33
illness, signs of 57
incontinence 114–15
injections 45
injuries
    car accidents 103
    health checks 56
insect stings 109
internet, researching breeds 16

J
Jack Russell Terrier 11
jackets, dog 61, 109, *109*
jealousy
    of new babies 13
    sibling rivalry 42, 121, *121*
joint problems 111
jumping up 23, 80
jumps, agility training 92–3, *92*

K
Kennel Club 77, 92, 97, 120
kennel cough 101
kennels
    boarding kennels 104–5
    outdoor 107, 109
kitchens, safety 34–5
Kong *91*

L
Labrador 91
leads 33

high-visibility *60*, 103
  lead training 74
  traffic safety 103
legs, health checks *45*
leptospirosis 101
licking 25, 113
lifespan 11, 111
lifting a puppy *38–9*
lightning, fear of 118, 119
living rooms, safety 35
long-haired dogs, choosing breeds 19
lost dogs 119
lungs, health checks *44*
Lurcher 28–9, 85
lying down
  down command 84–5, *84–5*
  relaxed dogs 64, *64*

M

male dogs, neutering 69, 112
manners, feeding time 50
markers, house-training 114
meals, routines 47
microchips 119
mounting, sexual behaviour 69, 112
mouth, health checks *44*
music
  heelwork to music (HTM) 96–7,
    96–7
  musical chairs 91
muzzle, sensitivity 73

N

nail clippers 52
names
  choosing 73
  learning 59
naughty dogs 68–9
neck, scruff of 45, 73
needles, injections 45
nervous dogs 25, 118–19
neutering 69, 112
nipping 23, 42
'no', saying 23, 42, 69
noise, nervous dogs 118–19
nose
  health checks 57
  smelling other dogs' bottoms 49

O

obedience training
  agility training 92–3, *92–3*
  classes 74
  stay command 83
obesity 111, 117

obstacle courses, agility training
  92–3
old dogs 111
outdoor dogs 28–9, *29*
overheating 108
  in cars 28, 104

P

pack animals, dogs as 63
pack leaders 68–9
pain, old dogs 111
parainfluenza 101
parasites
  in faeces 61
  fleas 33, 44, 45, 52, 100–1
  worms *45*, 99
parties 94–5, *94–5*
parvovirus 101
paws
  care of *53*
  chewing 113
  frostbite 108
  health checks *45*, 56
  high five trick 89
  shaking paws 89, *89*
  washing 109
pedigree dogs
  buying 20, 21
  choosing breeds 19
pet shops 21
pets, introducing puppy to 37
pheromones
  dog-appeasing pheromones (DAP) 119
  house-training 114
picnics 108
plants, poisonous 106
play 58–9, *58–9*
  games 90–1
  older dogs 111
  rewards 66
  safety 58
  time of day 41
poisonous plants 106
poop scoops 33
praise 67
puppies
  bathing 54–5, *54–5*
  bringing home 35, 36–7
  buying 20–1
  choosing breeds 19
  in family hierarchy 22–3, 69, 73
  feeding 50, *51*
  the first few days 33–45
  grooming 52–3, *52–3*
  house-training *10*, *37*, 107, 114–15

looking after 14–15
  needs 26–7
  play 58–9, *58–9*
  preparing for 19–31
  routines 47–61
  safe rooms 33, 34
  socializing 27, 31, 49
  training 63–71
  walking 60–1, *60*
  worming 99
puppy farms 21

R

races
  flyball 93
  at parties 95
rats, leptospirosis 101
rawhide chews 50
Ray, Mary *96*
relationships, child-dog 120–1
relaxed dogs 64–5
replacement dogs 123
rescue dogs
  choosing 16–17, 21
  house-training 114
research 16–17
rewards 66–7
  clicker training 76–7
road safety 102–3, *102–3*
roll over command 86, *86–7*
roundworms 99
routine, importance of 47
rubbish bins, scavenging 117
runs, outdoor 107

S

safe rooms 33, 34–5
safety
  bites 25
  in cars 104, 105
  clothing 60
  gardens 106–7
  kitchens 34–5
  living rooms 35
  play 58
  road safety 102–3, *102–3*
  summer hazards 108
  tricks 87
  in winter 109
  young children 70–1
  see also hygiene
scavenging 117
scissors 52
Scooby Doo 21
scruff of neck 45, 73

sea, swimming in 108
sexual behaviour 69, 112
shampoo 33, 54, *55*
shelter, outdoor dogs 28
shows, agility training 92
sibling rivalry 42–3, 121
sickness, eating grass 50
sit command 80, *80–1*
sit up and beg 88, *88*
size of dog, and dominance 73
sleep 40–1, *41*, 47
slicker brushes 52
smelly dogs 53
smiling 65
snacks 50
snow 108
socializing puppies 27, 31, 49
sports
    agility training 92–3, *92–3*
    flyball 93
    heelwork to music (HTM) 96–7
stair-gates 34, *34*
stand command 85
stay command 82–3, *82–3*
steel combs 52
stings, insect 109
storing food 33
storms, fear of 118, 119
strange dogs, approaching *24–5*
stressed dogs 22
stroking dogs 42, *42*, 67
submission 65
summer camps 77
summer hazards 108
swimming 91, 108

T
tails
    body language 65
    chasing 113
    wagging 25
tantrums, children 70
tapeworms 99
teenagers 120
teeth
    cleaning 56–7, *56–7*
    dry foods and 50
    health checks *44*, 56
    play biting 58
    teething 58
    toothbrushes and toothpaste 33, 52
temper tantrums 70
territory, urine marking 49
thunder, fear of 118, 119
ticks 101

time constraints, getting a dog 11
titbits 50
toilet training *10*, *37*, 107, 114–15
tolerance 30–1, 118
toothbrushes 33, 52
toothpaste 33, 52, *56–7*
top dogs *see* dominant dogs
towels 33, *55*
Toxascaris leonine 99
toxicariasis (toxocara) 99
Toxocara canis 99
toy dogs 19, 29
toys 33
    activity toys 91, *91*
    children's toys 113
    play 58
    as rewards 66
traffic
    introducing puppy to 49
    safety 102–3, *102–3*
training
    agility training 92–3, *92–3*
    clickers 33, 76–7, *76–7*
    coming back 78–9, *78–9*
    down command 84–5, *84–5*
    house-training *10*, *37*, 107, 114–15
    involving children 73–95
    lead training 74
    obedience classes 74
    puppies 63–71
    roll over command 86, *86–7*
    shaking paws 89, *89*
    sit command 80, *80–1*
    sit up and beg 88, *88*
    stay command 82–3, *82–3*
    traffic safety 102–3, *102–3*
    treats and rewards 66–7
    withdrawing treats 85
tranquillizers 119
travel
    in cars 104–5, *104–5*
    travelling boxes 34, *35*
treasure hunts 90, *90*
treats 66–7
    activity toys 91, *91*
    chocolate 27
    hiding 58–9
    in training 43
    treasure hunts 90, *90*
    waist bags 74
    and wind 50
    withdrawing in training 85
tricks 77
    high five 89
    at parties 95

roll over and die 86, *86–7*
safety 87
shaking paws 89, *89*
sit up and beg 88, *88*
tug-of-war 91
tunnels *93*

U V
urine
    house-training 37, 114–15
    marking territory 49
    smelly dogs 53
vaccinations 26, 44, 100–1, *100–1*, 107
verbal commands *43*
vets
    and behavioural problems 112
    euthanasia 123
    first visit to *27, 44–5*
    geriatric clinics 111
    house-training problems 115
    vaccinations 100–1
visitors, introducing puppy to 49
voice, tone of 67

W X Y
wagging tails 25
waist bags, for treats 74
wait command 80
walking 15, 60–1, *60*
    to heel 74, *75*
    traffic safety 102–3, *102–3*
warning signals 30
wasp stings 109
water
    drinking *26, 27, 107*, 108
    falling into icy water 109
    swimming 91, 108
    water bottles 108, *108*
weight, fat dogs 111, 117
wind 50
winter safety 109
worms *45*, 99
wriggling 39
Yorkshire Terrier 11, 61
zero-tolerance, bad behaviour 69, 71

Acknowledgements

Author acknowledgements

Many thanks to the primary school children – and their teachers – of Gonerby Hill Foot School, Grantham, for allowing me to chat to them and get a child's-eye view of what they think about dogs.

Thanks also to my lovely daughter, Madeline Joy Lainchbury, and her friends for their patience as I constantly picked their brains about what they thought was involved in looking after a dog. Their responses helped me uncover those areas of care that parents need most help in explaining.

I was invited to spend a day at a Young Kennel Club summer camp, where I was able to talk to trainers, parents and kids and was amazed at how knowledgeable and enthusiastic everyone was. It was inspirational to see so many children, teenagers and dogs enjoying themselves together and taking part in different activities.

Finally, thanks to my good friend Rick and his dog Oscar, who taught me a lot and made me smile in the process.

I'm grateful to you all for your help and advice in writing this book.

Photographic acknowledgements

Special Photography: © Octopus Publishing Group Limited/Russell Sadur.

Other photography: © Octopus Publishing Group Limited/Janeanne Gilchrist 96; /Steve Gorton 44–5; /Angus Murray/Steve Gorton 77 right.

Publisher acknowledgements

The publisher would like to thank all the children who were photographed for this book (and their parents and guardians for bringing them along): Alice Golding, Amelia Badenoch, Annie Weller, Cameron Thomson, Charlotte Ford, Charlotte Lee, Daniel Baxter, Ella Roscoe, Finlay Thomson, Fleur Bruneau-Cordell, Gabriella Turk, Greg Williams, James Golding, Jemma Austin, Kira Taylor, Leonardo Martini, Madeline Lainchbury, Nina Roscoe, Olivia Morrison, Phoebe Morrison, Polly Hardwicke, Rebecca Lawler, Sol Headley, Sophia Turk, Thomas Bruneau-Cordell, William Mason, Zara Williams. Thanks also to Sandra Strong and Jeanette Miller of Dogs on Camera.

Executive editor: Trevor Davies
Editor: Fiona Robertson
Executive art editors: Mark Stevens and
    Karen Sawyer
Designer: Mark Stevens
Photographer: Russell Sadur
Senior production controller: Martin Croshaw